W9-COB-171

Amazing Health Facts!

"Moses was one hundred and twenty years old when he died. His eyes were not dim nor his natural vigor abated." —Deuteronomy 34:7 (NKJV)

Even Moses had to die, but what a way to go! After living six score years, the weathered but wiry patriarch climbed a mountain. There, in the clean desert air and under blue skies, he viewed the Promised Land with crystal clear eyes. Then he simply lay down … and died.

During his pilgrimage in the wilderness, Moses followed all the Bible secrets for a longer, stronger life — fresh air, exercise, a good diet, and trust in God, just to name a few. Even though healthful living might not eliminate the prospect of death, it can certainly postpone it and greatly improve the quality of the life we do live!

Moses was active and lucid even on his last day: He "went up from the plains of Moab to Mount Nebo, to the top of Pisgah, which is across from Jericho" (Deuteronomy 34:1 NKJV).

It shouldn't take 10 years to die. One of the main reasons for America's health crisis is that through poor living habits, most people invite an unsavory assortment of disabling diseases. Plagued with a pandemic of diabetes, cancer, and heart disease, it seems that many people spend their last 10, 20, or even 30 years dying!

Moreover, these self-destructive lifestyles have led to overcrowded hospitals, astronomical medical costs, and a virtually bankrupt government. People are so stressed, they can't sleep, as antacids fly off the shelf and the number of handicap parking places seems to climb.

It doesn't need to be this way. It can change.

Indeed, people want good health … but they are clearly confused about where to find it.

According to the U.S. Food and Drug Administration, the public has 30,000 health supplements available to them on the market, representing a multibillion dollar industry. Indeed, more than 150 million Americans take some form of health supplement each year. Sadly, people are not only looking for health in all the wrong places, they're wasting a small fortune along the way.

Yet please consider that human physiology hasn't changed since the days of Moses, and those health secrets that worked for Moses also sustained an entire nation of people. In fact, after the Israelites traveled through the wilderness, following God's health plan along the way, the Bible records, "There was not one feeble person among their tribes" (Psalm 105:37).

Can you imagine that? A nation of more than 2 million citizens without one person in a clinic or nursing home! Likewise, it's not hard to fathom that 70 percent of our hospitals and pharmaceutical makers would simply shut down if we would all just follow the free health plan found in the Bible.

These Bible secrets of health — each summarized in this magazine — are not composed of mysterious rituals or strange herbal concoctions. They are real, proven principles backed by modern science. We only call them "secrets" here because they have been neglected and buried by time and culture.

So whatever your age, and regardless of your current health, these free principles can truly lead you to a longer and stronger … and happier … life.

If that is what you want, keep reading! ∎

Nutrition

In the beginning …
we ate our fruits and vegetables.

"God said, 'See, I have given you every herb that yields seed which is on the face of all the earth, and every tree whose fruit yields seed; to you it shall be for food" (Genesis 1:29 NKJV).

Amazing Health Fact

Born in 1483, Thomas Parr is said to have lived to the incredible age of 152! If true, that means he saw 10 sovereigns on the throne of England, including the entire 50-year reign of Queen Elizabeth I.

In 1635, King Charles I invited Parr to his palace and inquired as to how the old man managed to have such a long life. Parr answered that he had lived a simple life as a farmer, eating mostly potatoes, fruit, and oatmeal.

Unfortunately, "Old Parr" was not accustomed to the rich foods served at the palace. That night after dining, he became very ill — and died. King Charles felt so terrible for having killed Britain's oldest citizen with royal delicacies that he commanded Parr be buried in Westminster Abbey, where his grave can still be seen today.

It appears that Parr was living proof of the connection between a longer, stronger life and what you eat.

What was the original diet for humanity?

According to the Bible, after Creation, Adam and Eve were instructed to eat fruits, grains, and nuts. God also instructed them to eat vegetables: "You shall eat the herb of the field" (Genesis 3:18 NKJV). These were the original God-given dietary plans for those living up to the time of the Flood.

Following the Flood, due to the global obliteration of vegetation, a total plant-based diet was impossible for Noah and his family. In order to provide a consistent food source, God allowed for the eating of meat. However, God also designated the healthiest variety of animal for consumption, referring to these as "clean." (See Leviticus 11; Deuteronomy 14:3-21.) Of course, instead of going into the ark in pairs, clean animals went in by sevens!

Even though it was necessary at the time, meat eating apparently contributed to a tremendous decline in longevity. Before the Flood, human life spans remained steady at around 900 years (Genesis 5). After the Flood, we find that Noah's son Shem lived to be 600. Only nine generations later, Abraham lived to be just 175. Today, the average life expectancy is just a

Even though God permitted the eating of meat, He warned people not to eat meat that still has its lifeblood in it (Genesis 9:4, Leviticus 3:17, 1 Samuel 14:32–34). Indeed, some tribes in Africa, like the Maasai, consume blood as part of their diet. Autopsies performed on 50 Maasai men showed extensive heart disease. Though their extremely physical lifestyle offers some protection, they still have the worst life expectancy in the modern world (45 years for women and 42 years for men).

Post-Flood Lifespans

Age

1000	
900	
800	
700	
600	
500	
400	
300	
200	
100	
0	

Noah, Shem, Arphaxad, Shelah, Eber, Peleg, Reu, Serug, Nahor, Terah, Abraham

fraction of that of our pre-Flood ancestors. But if a diet rich in fruits, vegetables, nuts, seeds, and whole grains positively affected their longevity, could a return to the original diet extend our lives today?

Amazing Physiology

What follows the swallows?

A proper diet starts with proper digestion. Chewing food begins this process, so be sure to chew your food well! While food is still in the mouth, an enzyme (salivary amylase) begins to break it down.

Once swallowed, food is referred to as chyme. The chyme then makes its way down the esophagus and into the stomach, where stomach acid continues the complex chemical digestive process.

After this is complete, chyme passes into the small intestine, where a different enzyme breaks down carbohydrates. Bile is also secreted from the gallbladder to help digest fats, and the pancreas adds enzymes to further break it down too. The small intestine absorbs most of the nutrients as the chyme passes into the large intestine. At this point, digestion is mostly complete … and, well, you know the rest of the story.

Amazing Health Fact

The digestion process starts before you eat. It begins when you smell something irresistible or when you see a favorite food. The entire process of digestion will continue for the next 29 hours or so.

What do you need to know about nutrition?

The five basic components of food are carbohydrates, proteins, fats, vitamins, and minerals.

CARBOHYDRATES are sources of starches, sugars, and fiber. Starch and sugar are converted into glucose, which is the body's main fuel. Fiber, found primarily in plant foods, acts as a bulking agent that helps keep the intestines clean.

PROTEINS are broken down by the body and converted into amino acids, which are the building blocks for hormones, enzymes, and structural components of the body, such as muscle tissue.

FATS are the most concentrated form of energy, supplying over twice as many calories per gram than protein or carbohydrates. It can also be efficiently stored for later use. The three natural types of fats are monounsaturated, polyunsaturated, and saturated. The unsaturated fats are by far the healthiest form, especially when it comes from plant sources. Diets rich in refined saturated fats have been linked with numerous diseases.

VITAMINS AND MINERALS are essential components of our diet. Whole foods, which have been refined as little as possible, naturally contain the highest amount of these nutrients. Phytochemicals, found only in plants, are added bonuses thought to play a role in the prevention of many diseases.

Don't you need some cholesterol in your diet?

Cholesterol comes packaged in different ways. High density lipoprotein (HDL) is the healthy form of cholesterol and actually helps to remove bad cholesterol from the body, returning it to the liver for recycling. Here's a simple way to remember the good and bad of cholesterol: HDL is "healthy," LDL is "lousy," and VLDL is "very lousy."

Cholesterol is found only in meat and animal products, such as milk and eggs. However, newborn babies are the only humans who actually need a dietary source of cholesterol — which ideally comes

Amazing Health Fact

Did you know that skipping breakfast could be deadly? In one study, skipping breakfast was linked to an increased risk of premature death. By far, the best meal to skip or, at least minimize, is dinner. Another study reported better weight loss, improvement in diabetic conditions, and increased thyroid efficiency among a group of 595 people who consumed their last meal of the day by 3:00 PM.

from breast milk! Because of the liver's ability to produce cholesterol, we simply don't need a dietary source of cholesterol past breastfeeding age.

The Evidence

Research proves the connection between nutrition, health, and longevity.

Cardiovascular Disease: Is it harmful to have a little cholesterol here and there?

One of the most effective ways to reduce the risk of cardiovascular disease is following a cholesterol-free diet. In fact, one study found that consuming a balanced plant-based diet reduced the incidence of heart disease by 86 percent. Another scientific article pointed out that a total vegetarian (vegan) diet could prevent approximately 90 percent of all strokes and 97 percent of all heart attacks!

Indeed, research shows that consuming animal byproducts has a harmful effect on health. According to Dr. Hans Diehl, founder of CHIP, the Coronary Health Improvement Project, "The average risk of heart disease for a man eating meat, eggs, and dairy products is 45 percent.

The risk for a man who leaves off meat is 15 percent. However, the risk of a vegetarian who leaves off meat, eggs, and dairy products drops to only 4 percent."

Do some foods actually offer protection against heart disease?

Yes! It has been found that the "healthy fats" found in nuts and seeds can protect the heart. In one study, people who ate nuts at least five times a week lowered their risk of heart attack by 50 percent. Another study found that people who consumed high amounts of alpha-linolenic acid (found in walnuts) had an almost 50 percent reduction in the risk of a fatal heart attack. Studies also show that these fats might even prolong life among those who already suffer with heart disease.

Eating ample amounts of whole grains has also been found to reduce the risk of cardiovascular disease by up to 25 percent. In another finding, women who consumed the largest amount of whole grains had a 31 percent reduction in the incidence of stroke!

Finally, eating your fruits and vegetables can also protect you against heart disease. A study by the Harvard School of Public Health found that consuming leafy green vegetables

Amazing Health Fact

God knew what He was doing with the diet in Eden! Nuts contain the antioxidant vitamin E, folic acid (which reduces homocysteine levels), and plant fiber (which can reduce cholesterol levels). In addition, nuts contain arginine, a precursor to nitric acid, a substance made in the walls of blood vessels that prevents clotting.

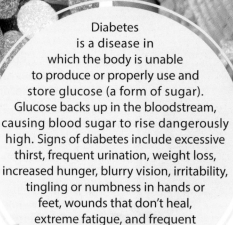

Amazing Health Fact

A U.S. Department of Agriculture study revealed that Americans eat an average of 32 teaspoons of sugar each day in their foods.

Diabetes is a disease in which the body is unable to produce or properly use and store glucose (a form of sugar). Glucose backs up in the bloodstream, causing blood sugar to rise dangerously high. Signs of diabetes include excessive thirst, frequent urination, weight loss, increased hunger, blurry vision, irritability, tingling or numbness in hands or feet, wounds that don't heal, extreme fatigue, and frequent skin, bladder, or gum infections.

reduced the risk of heart disease by 23 percent. Furthermore, those who consumed the largest amounts of fruits and vegetables had a 31 percent lower stroke risk. Fruits and vegetables are also naturally high in fiber, which has been shown to lower LDL (lousy) cholesterol.

Diabetes: Is it true that diabetes is caused by eating sugar?

If eating simple carbohydrates (highly refined foods, such as sugar) contributes to excess body weight, then yes, the risk of type 2 diabetes is increased. However, research has shown that consuming complex plant-based carbohydrates (food as grown) actually reduces the risk of developing diabetes. One study of 36,000 women in Iowa found that those who ate the largest amounts of unrefined carbohydrates and fiber had the least incidence of diabetes. Furthermore, a study conducted at the National Public Health Institute in Finland found that people who ate the largest quantity of whole grains had a 61 percent reduced risk of developing diabetes!

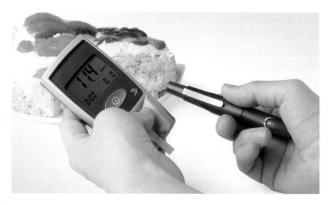

What about fat?

The two most significant risk factors in developing diabetes have to do with fat. Being overweight is one risk factor — but the most prominent factor is consuming large amounts of dietary fat. A study involving 1,300 Colorado residents determined that those with low-carbohydrate, high-fat diets were much more likely to develop diabetes. In another study of young men, researchers fed high-fat, low-carb diets to one group and a high-carb, low-fat diet to another. The group with the high-fat diet developed "chemical diabetes," but the low-fat group had no signs of diabetes by the conclusion of the study.

Eating highly refined foods has also been shown to increase the risk of developing diabetes. One study determined that consumption of partially hydrogenated oils is responsible for approximately 40 percent of all cases of type 2 diabetes in the United States!

Amazing Health Fact

God knew about fats. He commanded Israel to avoid bad fat — "Speak unto the children of Israel, saying, Ye shall eat no manner of fat, of ox, or of sheep, or of goat" (Leviticus 7:23).

Can type 2 diabetes be reversed with diet?

A total vegetarian diet not only prevents but can even reverse diabetes. In a study conducted at the world-renowned Pritikin Center, 40 medication-dependent diabetics were given a low-fat, plant-based diet combined

Amazing Health Fact

Once a viable and nutritious food source, excessive fish consumption has now been linked to heavy metal poisoning, cancer, birth defects, and numerous other diseases. Unfortunately, fish in even the cleanest waters are now contaminated with toxic substances such as mercury, PCBs, and DDT. This is due to the fact that fish absorb and concentrate toxins in their flesh.

American nurses found that those consuming red meat daily were 2.5 times more likely to develop colon cancer than those who consumed less than 1 serving per month.

Finally, numerous studies have shown the relationship between a high-sugar diet and cancer. High-sugar intake has been linked to an increased risk of cancers of the colon, rectum, breast, ovaries, uterus, prostate, kidney, as well as cancers of the central nervous system. One of the reasons suggested for sugar's effect on cancer is that sugar weakens the immune system. A study published by the Southern California Dental Association found that after consuming only 24 teaspoons of sugar, the ability of white blood cells to destroy bacteria was decreased by 92 percent!

Mental Health: Food for thought?

Not only is a meat and dairy diet a risk factor for cardiovascular disease, studies have actually shown that elevated levels of cholesterol can affect mental health. One study revealed that elevated levels of cholesterol are a significant factor in mild cognitive impairment.

Diet also plays a significant role in the development of Alzheimer's disease: Consuming large amounts of partially hydrogenated fats increases the risk of Alzheimer's by almost 2.5 times. Another study revealed that eating meat increased the diseases associated with Metabolic Syndrome, characterized by high insulin levels, which may also trigger Alzheimer's disease.

Foods in the Genesis diet are some of the best for preventing and fighting cancer! These include beans, berries, broccoli, cauliflower, cabbage, Brussels sprouts, bok choy, kale, dark green leafy vegetables, flaxseed, garlic, grapes and grape juice, soy beans, tomatoes, and whole grains.

with moderate exercise. Within 26 days of the start of the program, 34 participants were able to discontinue all diabetic medication!

WARNING! Do not stop your diabetes medication. Talk to your doctor first about your intention to invest in a good lifestyle.

Cancer: Does food impact your risk?

Fruits and vegetables are high in vitamins, fiber, and antioxidants — some of the best cancer-fighting ingredients that exist! In fact, one study found that men who eat three or more servings of cruciferous vegetables (broccoli, cauliflower, etc.) per week lowered their risk of prostate cancer by 41 percent. The World Cancer Research Fund found that people who consumed five or more servings of fruits and vegetables a day reduced cancer risk by approximately 50 percent. Vegetables, in particular, were found to help prevent cancers of the rectum and colon.

Conversely, diets rich in red meat and cholesterol have been linked to colon cancer. In fact, a study of 88,751

Obesity: Does the type of food you eat really affect weight gain?

It's a fact: The traditional Western diet leads to increased rates of obesity. Statistically, First World countries have dramatically higher rates of obesity than developing countries.

Indeed, an astounding 63 percent of American adults are overweight — and 26 percent are suffering obesity.

Unfortunately, children are also suffering. Research focusing on Japanese children has shown that an increase in meat and dairy product consumption increases childhood obesity by more than three times. The CDC also reports that approximately 13 percent of America's youth are overweight. Obese teens have a significantly shorter lifespan, dying at an average age of just 46! We also know today that people who are overweight have a significantly higher risk of developing diabetes, cancer, heart disease, stroke, high blood pressure, osteoarthritis, and other potentially serious diseases.

Amazing Health Fact

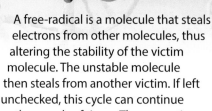

A free-radical is a molecule that steals electrons from other molecules, thus altering the stability of the victim molecule. The unstable molecule then steals from another victim. If left unchecked, this cycle can continue thousands of times. These reactions can damage DNA and lead to cellular reproduction disorders such as cancer. Antioxidants, such as the vitamins A, C, and E, have the power to stop this deadly cascade.

foods as the largest contributor. The average 12-ounce can of soda has 10 teaspoons of sugar — but even white bread contains roughly 3 teaspoons per slice!

Will "grazing" help you lose weight faster?

The term "grazing" refers to decreasing the size of meals while increasing the frequency. This approach has been suggested by weight loss "experts" as a logical approach to keep the body's blood sugar at steady levels throughout the day. However, such a diet

Can soft drinks contribute to a weight problem?

Yes, big time! Soft drinks are the largest source of sugar in the American diet. In fact, daily soft drink consumption adds roughly 9 teaspoons of sugar to the diet of adolescent girls and about 14 teaspoons for adolescent boys. According to the USDA, sugar consumption has been steadily increasing since 1982, with highly refined

Amazing Health Fact

Research backs the Bible: When taken captive, the ancient Bible prophet Daniel and his three friends requested "pulse" — things grown from seeds — to eat and water to drink. As a result, he and his friends, when tested by the king, were found to be 10 times smarter than the rest of the captives.

Amazing Health Fact

Supplementing a poor diet with vitamins and minerals does not reap the benefits of a naturally nutrient-rich diet. A study that looked at data from the First National Health and Nutrition Examination Survey showed that consuming dietary supplements (vitamins and minerals) had no impact upon longevity.

Eat for Strength ... and Enjoy It!

A plant-based diet might sound bland … but you can transition tastefully!

If you feel like the satisfaction of a meat diet could be worth the health risk, stop! Yes, a slice of tofu tastes different than a sirloin steak — but eating a plant-based diet doesn't have to be, and shouldn't be, a tasteless diet. Food was meant to be enjoyed! Fortunately, there are some great optimal-diet cookbooks to help you make the transition. (See page 45!) Living longer and stronger really is worth the investment!

can be harmful. Several studies have shown that snacking between meals increases the risk of developing colon cancer. The healthiest approach to stable blood sugar levels is to avoid highly refined foods and to increase your intake of dietary fiber.

Too much of a good thing …

Even an extremely healthy diet can be unhealthy: Overeating is the number one cause of obesity in the United States and has been linked to the development of numerous digestive disorders such as gastroesophageal reflux disorder, hiatal hernia, and cancers of the esophagus and stomach.

The Bread of Life

Complex carbohydrates, omega-3 acids, vitamins, minerals, phytonutrients, and a plant-based diet can give us a better quality of life and increase our longevity. However, we all will eventually face death. Yet if there was a food that promised to reverse the ravages of death and give eternal youth, would you eat it? There is only one "food" that promises such amazing results.

Jesus said, "I am the bread of life. He who comes to Me shall never hunger. … And the one who comes to Me I will by no means cast out" (John 6:35, 37 NKJV). What He said to His

Bread of Life

disciples 2,000 years ago, Jesus also says to you today.

Do you desire to come to Him? He has promised not to send you away hungry. Visit **www.AmazingHealthFacts.org** to discover more about nutrition and everlasting life. ■

Amazing Health Fact

Consumption of omega-3 fatty acids have been associated with decreased rates of depression and mental agitation.

Do Healthy Foods
Resemble the Body Parts
They Benefit?

*Adapted from David Bjerklie, *TIME*, October 2003

FOOD FILE

It seems like God might have given us visual cues to identify what parts of the body that many different fruits and vegetables benefit. Check out these uncanny resemblances …

A slice of **carrot** looks much like the pupil, iris, and radiating lines of the human eye. Of course, science has demonstrated that carrots improve eye function.

Tomatoes are a super food for the heart and blood. And like the human heart, the tomato is red and has four chambers!

Celery and **rhubarb** look just like bones, and each helps bone strength. Bones are 23 percent sodium, and so are celery and rhubarb! If you don't have enough sodium in your diet, the body pulls it from the bones, making them weak. These foods replenish the skeletal needs of the body!

A shelled **walnut** looks like a little brain, with a left and right hemisphere, upper cerebrums, lower cerebellums, and even the wrinkles and folds of the neo-cortex! We now know that walnuts are great brain food.

Eggplant and **avocados** resemble the womb and cervix. Research shows that when a woman eats one avocado a week, it balances hormones, sheds unwanted birth weight, and prevents cervical cancer. Amazingly, it takes exactly nine months for an avocado to grow from blossom to ripened fruit!

Kidney beans were named thus because they look so much like the human organ, and they actually do help heal the kidneys and maintain their function!

Grapes hang in heart-shaped clusters and look like blood cells. Research today shows that grapes are indeed a profound heart- and blood-vitalizing food.

Exercise

In the beginning … life was active.

: *"The LORD God took the man and put*
: *him in the garden of Eden to tend and*
: *keep it" (Genesis 2:15 NKJV).*

When Wilma Rudolph was only four years old, she contracted polio, which left her with a paralyzed leg. Her doctors said she'd never walk without assistance.

But Wilma did not give up, determined to exercise her crippled limb. At age nine, she stunned doctors when she removed her metal leg brace and began to walk without it.

When she was 13, Wilma decided to become a runner. She entered a race and came in last. For the next few years, every race she entered, she came in last. Everyone told her to quit, but she kept on. Then one day, she won a race … and then another … and then every race she entered. Eventually, she went on to win three Olympic gold medals in track and field!

Wilma chose activity over atrophy and became a winner. Likewise, your body is a miraculous machine, but if you don't use it, you'll lose it.

What was the original exercise routine?

When Adam was in the garden of Eden, he had perfect exercise habits. (Indeed, gardening can be a very effective total body workout!) However, things didn't stay perfect — sin brought with it the realities of disease and death.

And, according to the Bible, mankind's original workout routine had also changed. Just as a fitness trainer makes changes to an exercise program, God needed to make changes to Adam's exercise routine: "Cursed is the ground for your sake; In toil you shall eat of it All the days of your life. …

In the sweat of your face you shall eat bread" (Genesis 3:17, 19 NKJV). Adam's "workout" was now more difficult, because he had to "toil" and "sweat."

But take a closer look at this passage: This increase in Adam's exercise intensity was "for [his] sake." Could there still be life-giving benefits in "toil and sweat" exercise?

Amazing Physiology

What happens to the body during exercise?

Exercise is essential to good health, and the entire body is affected. Muscle fibers contract and release, the heart pumps more rapidly, and the lungs work harder to get more oxygen to the body. These actions trigger increased enzyme reactions, nerve stimulations, metabolic enhancement, and more. Exercise is an awesome event!

Why do you need a good workout?

Exercise can help you to:

- burn calories,
- increase strength & endurance,
- feel better & have more energy
- optimize heart health,
- and live a longer, happier life!

And all these goals can be accomplished with even a basic understanding of exercise physiology.

What is the best exercise routine?

Did you know there are two different types of muscles? Muscles involved in anaerobic (needing minimal oxygen) exercise are known as "fast twitch" muscles. To increase your strength, these muscles must be challenged with a task they haven't been required to accomplish before. These muscles "learn," enlarging to strengthen in case they run into the same task again. Weight training that focuses on lifting heavier weights with less frequency targets these muscles.

"Slow twitch" muscles are responsible for endurance activities and are used in aerobic (needing lots of oxygen) exercise. Although they don't "bulk up," they are responsible for significant calorie burning.

The best fitness program exercises both of these muscle types. A routine that features endurance *and* strength training will boost metabolism, burn fat, strengthen the cardiovascular system, and more!

How do I target heart health?

Heart fitness is best achieved through exercise that keeps your heart rate within age-specific parameters — your "target heart rate." Your specific rate can be calculated using this formula:

- 220 - (Your age) = target heart rate in beats per minute.

For example, the target heart rate for a 40-year-old is 180 beats per minute. (220 - 40 = 180 beats per minute.)

To get your heart as healthy as possible, your pulse rate needs to stay between 50 to 75 percent of your target rate during sustained aerobic activity.

Confused about target heart rate? Let's talk …

If you don't feel comfortable calculating your target heart rate or taking your pulse, try the "conversational heart rate" approach. If you can exercise and carry on a basic conversation, you are probably exercising in your target zone. But if you can sing while you exercise, you probably are not exercising hard enough. If you are winded and have to take breaks to catch your breath

Amazing Health Fact

Use it; don't eat it. Red meat is red because it is primarily composed of type II muscle fibers, which require a large amount of oxygen-rich blood. Studies have shown that consuming red meat actually increases the risk of cardiovascular disease and colon cancer.

between words, you probably are exercising too hard. This method works best for moderate intensity exercises, such as walking.

What if my main goal is to lose weight?

If you want to lose weight, remember this important equation: Calories going in must be less than calories lost. In other words, to lose weight, your energy expenditure must be more than the number of calories you eat.

Did you know that your body is constantly burning calories, even while sleeping? The rate at which your body uses calories simply to stay alive is known as "basal metabolic rate" (BMR). Studies have shown that building more muscle mass, through weight training, actually increases BMR — which means your body will naturally burn more calories in a day.

Aerobic exercise, like brisk walking, will burn additional calories per hour on top of your BMR. So a regular exercise routine that alternates between aerobic and anaerobic exercise is best for sustained weight loss.

Another important consideration for burning fat is exercise intensity: It should be moderate, not intense. During moderate exercise, fat is used as energy, but during intense exercise, carbohydrate (glucose) becomes the fuel of choice.

How can I get enough exercise with my busy schedule?

You might find it easier to simply start the day earlier with exercise. Experts believe that the early morning is the optimal time to exercise because air quality is generally better then. Plus, follow through with an exercise routine has been shown to be greater for those exercising in the morning.

What is the all-around best aerobic exercise?

Thomas Jefferson once said, "The sovereign invigorator of the body is exercise, and of all exercises walking is the best." Although not the most intense exercise, brisk walking might be the most effective. Walking is also a "low impact" exercise, meaning that there is a lower risk for injury and less of a shock to the joints, particularly the knees, when compared to running. Not only does walking work every major muscle group, many people make it a social event. (In fact, any exercise is benefited by having a partner.) Walking is also the least expensive exercise available: All you need is a comfortable pair of shoes.

Too much of a good thing …

Increasing your exercise intensity should be a gradual process. In fact, for those living a sedentary lifestyle, a sudden high intensity workout can be deadly. In one study, researchers estimated that almost half of all heart attacks are triggered by strenuous physical effort. The

Intermittent Training (IT) is an exercise style characterized by intense activity followed by a short period of rest. Researchers have found that this type of exercise is able to increase aerobic capacity (the amount of oxygen your body can use) and reduce fatigue better than sustained exercise.

study found that those who were less active were at much greater risk for a heart attack following strenuous exercise than those on a regular exercise routine.

PLEASE NOTE: Check with your doctor before beginning a new exercise program!

The Evidence

Research firmly proves the connection between exercise, health, and longevity.

Cardiovascular Disease: What types of exercise can prevent heart disease?

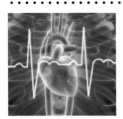

Men who engage in regular physical activity have a significantly reduced risk of developing heart disease. A study conducted by the Harvard School of Public Health found that running more than an hour per week decreased the risk of heart disease by 42 percent.

Walking 30 minutes a day or more reduced the risk of heart disease by 18 percent as well. Researchers also noticed a connection between the pace of walking and heart disease: The more intense the workout, the smaller the risk. Plus, weight training also has a preventative effect: 30 minutes or more of weight training per week means a 23 percent heart disease risk reduction.

For women, those who walked more than one hour per week had a 50 percent reduced risk of developing heart disease than women who walked less frequently. However, the study found that exercise intensity for women had less impact on the rate of heart disease than the duration of exercise.

What about exercise and stroke?

A study that examined the lifestyle patterns of 1,130 Harvard alumni found that moderate exercise also decreased the risk of stroke. Those who burned between 2,000 and 2,999 calories per week saw a total reduction in stroke risk of 46 percent! Researchers cited walking as a very effective form of exercise for stroke risk reduction. In fact, they found that walking more than 12 miles per week decreased the risk of stroke by 29 percent.

Cancer: What types of cancer are affected by exercise?

The preventative effects of regular exercise against cancer appear to be gender specific …

For Men: One study found that regular exercise decreased prostate cancer risk by around 74 percent. Numerous studies have also shown the relationship between regular exercise and a lowered risk of colon cancer. In one study, men who worked in sedentary jobs had a 60 percent increase in the development of colon cancer. (Many studies suggest that exercise has a smaller effect against colon cancer for women.)

For Women: Regular exercise is linked to a decreased risk of breast cancer and other female-specific cancers. According to one study, the risk of developing breast cancer was decreased 37 percent by regular exercise. Moreover, another study discovered that when women already afflicted with breast cancer walked between 6 to 8 hours a week, they decreased their risk of early death by 50 percent. One study also found that female former college athletes were less likely to develop cancer of the breast, uterus, ovaries, vagina, and cervix as well.

Obesity: Can exercise really help lose the extra weight?

One of the risk factors for developing obesity is a sedentary lifestyle. For weight loss to occur, remember that energy output must be greater than energy intake — and the best way to increase energy output is exercise.

Plus, regular moderate exercise is also important in sustaining weight loss. A study by the National Weight Control Registry found that 91 percent of those who had sustained weight loss followed a regular exercise routine, such as an hour of brisk walking each day.

Amazing Health Fact

Moderate exercise can improve memory and concentration among the elderly and has been linked with improved cognitive performance in Alzheimer's disease.

Diabetes: Does exercise have sweet rewards for diabetes prevention?

One study that compared metformin, a diabetes medication, versus regular moderate exercise showed that lifestyle change was far superior in preventing the onset of diabetes. A group of people with pre-diabetic conditions was studied: Those taking metformin had a 31 percent reduction in the risk of developing diabetes. However, regular moderate exercise cut the risk by 58 percent! (Results for those 60 years and older were even more dramatic: 71 percent.) Plus, those who exercised their way to diabetes prevention had the bonus of missing out on the usual side effects of metformin — loss of appetite, nausea and vomiting, indigestion, and diarrhea.

Can exercise also reverse diabetes?

Lifestyle centers, such as the Weimar Center of Health & Education in California, have had tremendous success in reversing diabetes. These physician-monitored programs stress health education, exercise, a healthy diet, and other lifestyle factors helpful in reaching optimal health.

Studies have shown that exercise in particular has an immediate and prolonged effect on blood sugar among diabetics. One study reported that the benefits of increased glucose usage lasted several hours after exercise. Another study revealed that the body's own insulin, which suffers from impaired function among type 2 diabetics, actually improved in function for up to 16 hours following moderate exercise.

PLEASE NOTE: If you are taking diabetes medication, check first with your physician before beginning any exercise program.

Amazing Health Fact

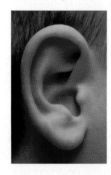

Did you know that exercise is good for your ears? One study found that participants in the Alameda County Health Study who exercised regularly had less incidence of hearing loss. The study also found that the overall rate of hearing loss had doubled between 1965 and 1994: even more reason to shout about the benefits of exercise!

Mental Health: Can exercise help you think more clearly?

According to researchers at the National Institute of Mental Health, regular exercise increases feelings of well-being, reduces stress (anxiety and tension), offers long-term anxiety relief, eases depression, while reducing muscle tension, heart rate, and certain stress hormones.

How does exercise boost your mental performance?

The positive benefits of exercise in blood circulation also help improve mental health. Exercise significantly improves blood flow to the brain and increases brain neurotransmitters, such as serotonin and dopamine, which have a positive effect on mood and well-being.

Osteoporosis: Can exercise contribute to strong bones?

Osteoporosis can be prevented and even reversed by "weight bearing" exercises, meaning an application of force to the bones beyond that which is regularly applied. Therefore, swimming, while a great exercise for the heart and muscles, is not as effective as building bone density in the legs and hips like walking, jogging, and cycling.

However, whole body bone density requires a whole body weight-bearing routine. Studies show that a balanced weight training routine is one of the most effective ways to build bone density. One study reported that yard work (a combination of raking, weeding, gardening, etc.) was just as effective in building whole body bone density as a weight training routine!

20
40
60
80
100

Arthritis: Can exercise help with your aches and pains?

Exercise can help relieve arthritis pain, but you must follow a regular routine to see improvement. One study found that moderate exercise helped lessen symptoms of osteoarthritis in people over 60. Those in the study who adhered to the recommended exercise routine showed the greatest decrease in pain and flexibility issues.

Exercise of a Different Variety

As you have seen, we need to exercise routinely to promote good health and prevent disease. But there is another form of exercise that yields even greater rewards:

"Bodily exercise profits a little, but godliness is profitable for all things, having promise of the life that now is and of that which is to come" (1 Timothy 4:8 NKJV).

Just as we must exercise to promote bodily health, we must exercise to receive spiritual health. To reach this goal, we are to exercise faith. One writer put it this way:

"Let us lay aside every weight, and the sin which so easily ensnares us, and let us run with endurance the race that is set before us, looking unto Jesus, the author and finisher of our faith, who for the joy that was set before Him endured the cross, despising the shame, and has sat down at the right hand of the throne of God" (Hebrews 12:1, 2 NKJV).

Would you like to lay down the burdens in your life? "Those who wait on the LORD Shall renew their strength; They shall mount up with wings like eagles, They shall run and not be weary" (Isaiah 40:31).

That's good advice, both physically and spiritually — so why not start an exercise program as soon as possible? Visit **www.AmazingHealthFacts.org** for more about physical and spiritual exercise. ■

Water

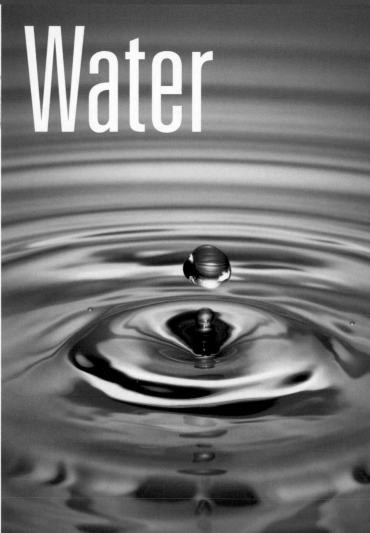

In the beginning … water was everywhere.

"Now a river went out of Eden to water the garden, and from there it parted and became four riverheads" (Genesis 2:10 NKJV).

About 100 years ago, a pile of bones was found on a sand dune in Saudi Arabia. Evidently, a man had died while lost in the desert. In one of the pockets of his tattered clothes was a scribbled note that read, "Dying of thirst. I cannot go on any longer." The lost soul had apparently assembled a small makeshift shelter there and, without water, sat down to die. Tragically, his remains were found right across a sand dune from a lush oasis — dying from thirst only a few hundred yards from artesian springs.

In a similar way today, millions are slowly dying from dehydration while surrounded by the most important, basic, and abundant substance on earth: water!

Did God Plan Ahead?

"The LORD God had not caused it to rain on the earth, and there was no man to till the ground; but a mist went up from the earth and watered the whole face of the ground. And the LORD God formed man of the dust of the ground (Genesis 2:5–7 NKJV).

The Bible records that even before plants, animals, or mankind ever experienced thirst, God had already supplied their need by creating plenty of water. Could it be possible that God's prescription for thirst is still valid today? Let's reexamine the vital life-giving properties of water, a substance we often take for granted …

Amazing Physiology

How much water do our bodies contain?

Water is found everywhere in our body, from the aorta (the largest blood vessel in our body) to the zygoma (a bone in the skull). Our bodies consist of more than 60 percent water by weight.

Plus, certain tissues and organs have even higher concentrations of water. The brain is about 70 percent water, and the lungs contain even more: up to 90 percent!

We not only use water to clean the outside of our bodies, but the inside as well. Even on the microscopic level, water is a cleansing agent and referred to as the

"universal solvent." Many compounds can be dissolved in water and thus put into solution. Blood, for example, is approximately 83 percent water. The remaining percent consists of blood cells, nutrients, hormones, etc.

Without adequate water, our blood would become concentrated. To give you a picture of what would happen: Imagine washing dishes with concentrated orange juice mix. You'd have a very sticky situation!

What happens to our bodies when we don't have enough water?

Our bodies have an intricate defense mechanism to protect vital organs from periods of inadequate water. The body takes water from less vital areas (skin, joints, bones, etc.) and gives it to the brain, heart, and other organs.

Unfortunately, many people live their entire lives in this partially dehydrated condition — resulting in premature aging, stress on kidneys, arthritis, and a host of other health problems.

How much water do we really need?

It is important to drink water regularly and consistently, even long before you feel thirsty.

The following recommendations, from the World Health Organization (WHO), are for *daily* water intake under normal environmental conditions:

FEMALES: Approximately nine 8-ounce glasses
MALES: Approximately twelve 8-ounce glasses

On average, 4 percent of the body's water is lost per day. Water is lost through urine, bowel movements, sweating, and breathing. Of course, copious sweating and breathing from exercise will necessitate additional water intake slightly above these recommendations.

Why can't we just drink water when we're thirsty?

Do you wait to drink water until you feel thirsty? According to experts, you are probably suffering from dehydration (too little water) long before your brain tells you to drink something.

What are some of the early symptoms of dehydration?

Mild dehydration is a 1 to 3 percent reduction in body weight as a result of fluid loss and can cause:

- headache,
- fatigue,
- confusion,
- loss of appetite,
- flushed skin,
- heat intolerance,
- light-headedness,
- dry mouth and eyes,
- lack of skin elasticity,
- stomach pains, which could be confused as hunger,
- and a slower metabolism, which can result in weight gain.

Amazing Health Fact

Simple filtration, reverse osmosis, and steam distillation are some of the methods commercial water suppliers use to purify water. Some also add minerals to improve taste. One way to improve the taste of your drinking water is to add a squeeze of fresh lemon or lime juice.

those hospitalized with dehydration, an estimated 18 percent will die within 30 days despite medical treatment. Of course, this is even more of a concern in hotter and dryer climates.

Is it really that easy to become dehydrated?

It is very easy to become dehydrated. Going one day without adequate water can cause moderate dehydration. Going two days without water could result in a life-threatening case of dehydration.

What's the relationship between water and blood sugar?

Water is the original "zero-calorie" beverage. Because it contains no sugar to raise blood glucose levels, it is the perfect choice for diabetics. Did you know that, in general, increased blood sugar causes an increased thirst sensation? The next time you overeat, determine if you become very thirsty shortly after finishing the meal. This is your body's way of diluting the concentration of sugar by demanding an increase of water in the bloodstream. This process can result in frequent urination and even high blood pressure.

Can dehydration be more serious?

Absolutely. If unchecked, dehydration can lead to a worsening of these symptoms and can progress to heat exhaustion, characterized by nausea and vomiting, which will in turn make dehydration worse. And it can happen very quickly. Severe dehydration is life-threatening!

Too much of a good thing?

Drinking too much water is rare, but it can happen. Forcing yourself to drink massive amounts of water can cause low blood sodium levels and lead to brain swelling and even death. In fact, years ago, the U.S. Army lost a number of soldiers to this condition. In 1998, they issued guidelines to prevent dangerously excessive water intake: roughly less than six 8-ounce glasses per hour and no more than 50 per day.

Are older people more susceptible to dehydration?

Because of changes in the body that accompany aging, combined with a diminished thirst sensation, elderly people are at much higher risk for dehydration.

In fact, severe dehydration is one of the primary reasons for hospitalizations. This problem seems to increase with age, as one study revealed that the age group over 85 years old is six times more likely to be hospitalized for dehydration than those aged 65 to 69. And dehydration in the elderly can easily progress to an untreatable state: Among

The Evidence

Research proves the connection between water intake, health, and longevity.

Cardiovascular Disease: Can water help your heart?

A recent study that included more than 20,000 participants discovered that men who drank more than five 8-ounce glasses of water a day cut their risk of heart disease by 46 percent. The number was even greater for women: 59 percent!

Hypotension: Water to the rescue?

One study found that individuals with orthostatic hypotension (low blood pressure when standing up from a seated position) were able to tolerate position changes after drinking one to two glasses of water. Water seems to have an unexplainable vasopressor effect, meaning that the absorption of water into the bloodstream was not the main cause of the increase in blood pressure. (Don't worry — consuming water is not linked to high blood pressure!)

Amazing Health Fact

Unless you are proactive in your daily intake of water, dehydration could become a way of life. It is little wonder that 75 percent of Americans are chronically dehydrated. In 37 percent, the thirst sensation is so impaired, it is mistaken for feelings of hunger.

Cancer: Can water make a difference in cancer prevention?

Adequate water intake has an incredible preventative effect on colon cancer. One study reported that adequate water intake reduced the incidence of colon cancer in men by 92 percent. Another study found that postmenopausal women who drank more than five glasses of water a day lowered their risk of breast cancer by 79 percent. Research has also shown that individuals can lower their risk of bladder cancer by 51 percent simply by drinking enough water.

Amazing Health Facts

Drinking other beverages (fruit juice, coffee, tea, etc.) does not provide the same health benefits as plain water. In fact, research has shown that women who consume large quantities of non-water beverages increased their risk of a fatal heart attack by two-and-a-half times. The same study showed that men increased their risk by 50 percent!

Hydrotherapy, or water therapy, can also treat arthritis pains. Hydrotherapy uses hot and cold water treatments to achieve a "push and pull" effect upon the body's circulatory system. Thus, it can stimulate blood flow to undernourished arthritic joints.

Obesity: Can water burn unwanted calories?

A study to determine water's effect on metabolism discovered that, after drinking about two glasses of water, participants' metabolic rates increased by an average of 30 percent. The change in metabolism started after 10 minutes and lasted over an hour! The surveyors believe that an increase in water intake of six glasses per day has the potential to burn the energy equivalent of about five pounds of fat per year.

Urinary Tract Health: Is more water (and bathroom breaks!) really necessary?

Your kidneys are sophisticated filters that process about 200 quarts of blood each day to sift out about two quarts of waste products. The only substance that properly cleans the kidneys is water. According to the National Kidney Research Fund, increasing water intake to approximately eight glasses a day is the best way to ensure proper kidney function, avoid kidney stones, flush impurities from the blood, and protect against urinary tract infections.

Arthritis/Joint Pain: Can water help with your aches and pains?

Drinking adequate water every day can significantly ease back and joint pain. Your joints are cushioned by fluid-filled sacs, but when you are dehydrated, your body draws water from these non-essential areas to supply water to more vital areas. As a result, joints are not adequately cushioned and movement can become painful. In fact, moderate and severe dehydration can actually mimic arthritic conditions!

Digestive Health: Does water help or hinder digestion?

Here are some additional hydration suggestions from physicians at the Weimar Center of Health & Education:

- Drink large amounts of warm water in the morning to flush your digestive system and reduce the risk of constipation.

- Drink purified or distilled water when possible.

- Drink between meals to ensure optimal digestion; it is best to abstain from water about a half hour before meals and one hour after eating. Too much water during meals will dilute stomach enzymes and interrupt the digestion process.

Moisturize your IQ

Water plays an extremely important role in brain function. It is vital to energy production in your cells and neurotransmission. Small waterways, or micro-streams, run along the full length of your nerves. These streams float the neurotransmitters along microtubules to the nerve endings. When your body is dehydrated, nerve transmission is compromised and brain function is diminished. Foggy thinking can be the result of a dry brain!

Amazing Health Fact

About 83 percent of your blood is water. If that ratio drops just 5 percent, you will no longer be able to see. Another 10 percent and you will be unable to hear. A 12 percent reduction leads to your blood thickening, making it impossible for your heart to pump it, which leads to death. On the other hand, a camel can lose 40 percent of the water content in its blood and do just fine!

Amazing Health Fact

Water can help keep your gallbladder clean. In a recent study, researchers found that drinking adequate room-temperature water resulted in gallbladder emptying. Furthermore, low daily water intake has been cited as a factor in the formation of gallstones … just one more reason to drink plenty of water.

Water Inside and Out

You've seen the many health benefits of water on the inside, but don't neglect its benefits on the outside. External cleanliness is perhaps the greatest health advancement made in modern history. In the 1860s, Dr. Joseph Lister read in the Bible that Moses told the Jews to wash with water after touching anything unclean (Leviticus 22:6). But when Lister suggested surgeons wash their hands and medical instruments before operating, he was mocked as eccentric. Yet death from infection dropped 75 percent in his hospital, and Lister's advice soon became the standard. Daily washing of the body and frequent washing of the hands can help prevent a virtual encyclopedia of ills.

"For He draws up drops of water, Which distill as rain from the mist, Which the clouds drop down And pour abundantly on man" (Job 36:27–29).

Living Water

As important as water is to our health, something else is even more important: Jesus is called the Living Water who provides eternal life. In the same way that many people go through life chronically dehydrated, many more go through life spiritually dehydrated. Like the altered thirst sensation that many mistake

as hunger, many mistakenly discern spiritual thirst for hunger after the things of this world.

Speaking of water, Jesus said, "Whoever drinks of this water will thirst again, but whoever drinks of the water that I shall give him will never thirst. But the water that I shall give him will become in him a fountain of water springing up into everlasting life" (John 4:13, 14 NKJV). And this offer was for anyone, including you: "Let him who thirsts come ... let him take the water of life freely" (Revelation 22:17 NKJV).

To learn more about this water that will never leave you thirsty again, visit **www.AmazingHealthFacts.org.** ■

Sunlight

In the beginning …
light was good.

: *"Then God said, 'Let there be light'; and
: there was light. And God saw the light,
: that it was good" (Genesis 1:3, 4 NKJV).*

The sun is a colossally big, fantastically hot cosmic radiation powerhouse with a surface temperature of about 11,000 degrees Fahrenheit. Its interior temperature is a little warmer — *estimated as high as 18 million degrees!*

The pressure at the center of the sun is about 700 million tons per square inch. It's enough to smash atoms and create nuclear fusion at the sun's core, allowing it to give off constant light and warmth. In fact, the material at its core is so hot that if you could capture enough to cover a pinhead, it would radiate so much heat it would kill a person one mile away.

Fortunately, earth is safely positioned about 93 million miles away, meaning it takes the light of the sun about 8 minutes and 20 seconds to reach our world. Just in time to do a lot of good.

What's so good about light?

Light is essential to all life — so essential that God provided the sun as a constant source to supply the energy necessary to sustain all life on earth. The energy used by plants growing in your garden, a cheetah running at top speed, and even the gasoline that powers your car can all be traced back to the energy supplied by sunlight. In fact, solar power is the originator of nearly all naturally occurring energy on the earth.

Yet even though God said that light was good in the beginning, many people are actually afraid of sun exposure today. Perhaps we have been so misinformed, we are overreacting to the dangers of sunlight while missing the many positive health benefits. "Truly the light is sweet, and a pleasant thing it is for the eyes to behold the sun" (Ecclesiastes 11:7).

Amazing Physiology

Can sunlight actually improve health?

Like plants, human beings also need sunlight for optimal health. Although many believe that any exposure to sunlight is harmful, it is actually an overexposure to direct sunlight that should be avoided.

In fact, in moderation, sunlight can …

- ease tension,
- increase immunity,
- prevent diseases,
- improve sleep,
- increase mental performance,
- heighten metabolism,
- relieve arthritic pains,
- and boost energy levels.

Many of sunlight's benefits are connected to vitamin D. Our bodies must have the UVB radiation found in sunlight to make this essential, health-promoting vitamin.

When exposed to sunlight, our skin begins to protect itself from overexposure by producing melanin, a chemical that darkens skin, and vitamin D precursors. Increased melanin and vitamin D allow increased exposure to the sun without burning.

How much sun exposure do I need?

Approximately 30 minutes a day, 3 times a week, in direct sunlight is adequate for most Caucasians. The darker your skin, the more sun exposure you need to obtain an adequate amount of vitamin D. However, if you have very fair skin, burn easily, or live in areas where the sun is particularly intense, you will want to make sun exposure a gradual process. If reddening of the skin occurs, you may have spent too much time in the sun!

Start with as little as five minutes per day (for the fair-skinned) and gradually increase exposure to 30 minutes or more per day. If you stay out in the sun for longer periods of time, be sure to wear a wide-brimmed hat and clothes that will protect the areas of your body that are most likely to get burned (face, ears, neck, shoulders, and back). Be aware, however, that barriers that reduce ultraviolet (UV) radiation (sunscreen, windows, etc.) also will reduce vitamin D production in your body!

Too much of a good thing …

Remember, sunlight is best in moderation. Protein and genetic tissue are damaged each time your skin burns, putting you at greater risk for skin cancer.

However, don't let this scare you away from obtaining proper sun exposure! The body will make adequate vitamin D with only one quarter of the sunlight required to cause a sunburn.

And although skin cancer claims the lives of approximately 2,000 Americans per year, researchers believe that regular, moderate exposure to the sun can actually prevent 138,000 deaths from other types of cancer each year.

The Evidence

Research proves the connection between sunlight exposure, health, and longevity.

Cardiovascular Disease: Can sunlight help your heart?

According to nutrition experts, vitamin D helps the intestines more efficiently absorb calcium and phosphorus — elements that can lower high blood pressure. (High blood pressure has been linked with serious complications such as heart disease, heart attacks, and strokes.)

In fact, researchers from Harvard University published a study looking at the correlation between vitamin D levels and heart disease. The results were startling: Those with inadequate vitamin D had more than twice the risk for heart attacks than those with optimal levels!

Amazing Health Facts

More than 90 percent of Americans are vitamin D deficient.

The National Institutes of Health reports that 10 to 15 minutes of sunlight allow adequate time for vitamin D synthesis to occur.

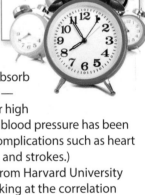

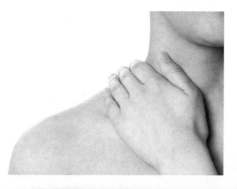

risk of obesity. The study also showed that kidney function was significantly increased by good levels of vitamin D.

Obesity: Can sunlight ward off obesity?

One advantage of moderate sunlight exposure is that it increases the production of serotonin, the "feel good" hormone. But besides being produced by sunlight exposure, serotonin is elevated significantly by eating excessive amounts of refined carbohydrates, such as ice cream and snack cakes. However, diets high in refined carbohydrates have been linked with a significantly increased risk of obesity, so it's healthier to get your serotonin by sunlight rather than junk food!

Cancer: Can sunlight actually prevent cancer?

Exposure to sunlight has also been found to prevent certain cancers. One study concluded that moderate sunlight exposure decreased colon cancer risk by up to 80 percent. Indeed, vitamin D is believed to actually stop a variety of cancer cells from growing — including leukemia, lymphoma, and melanoma (skin cancer).

Amazing Health Fact

It has been estimated that moderate sunlight exposure decreases breast cancer rates by as much as 50 percent!

Diabetes: How does sunlight affect diabetes?

Vitamin D also has an incredible preventative effect against juvenile diabetes. One study found that children in Finland given a vitamin D supplement had an 88 percent less chance to develop type 1 diabetes. (This study was done in Finland because of the limited sunlight the nation's children receive nine months out of the year. Vitamin D supplements are not necessary for a child who receives adequate sun exposure.)

Another study of American adults showed a benefit of adequate sunlight exposure on numerous type 2 diabetes risk factors. Most notably, adequate intake of vitamin D reduced the

Osteoporosis: Can sunlight reach our bones?

Vitamin D is very important for bone health. In one French study, researchers reported that calcium and vitamin D reduced the risk of hip fractures by 43 percent! (The study focused on women aged 78 to 90, a high-risk group for osteoporosis.) Furthermore, adequate vitamin D levels, along with sufficient dietary calcium, have been shown to increase bone density in people who are prone to osteoporosis.

Amazing Health Fact

Sunscreens with sun protection (SPF) of 8 or greater will block ultraviolet rays that produce vitamin D.

Sunlight exposure can prevent falls!

Amazingly, vitamin D, which can be obtained through sunlight exposure, has been linked to a significant reduction in the risk for falls. One study showed that, among 246 older women, those who had adequate vitamin D and calcium reduced their chances of falling by up to 66 percent. The strengthening effect of vitamin D upon muscle tissue was cited as being the most likely contributor to the reduction in risk.

Skin Health: Isn't sunlight bad for our skin?

Sunlight is antibacterial, antiviral, and antifungal. Thus it's absolutely beneficial for certain skin conditions, such as acne, athlete's foot, viral skin infections, and more.

But remember three important considerations for sunlight and skin health: moderation, moderation, moderation. Frequent and excessive tanning can cause skin to dry, wrinkle, and prematurely age. So if you want to be good to your skin, be sure avoid overexposure *and* underexposure!

Sleep Disorders: How can sunshine help you sleep better?

Believe it or not — sunlight can help you sleep better at night. When sunlight enters the retina of your eye, it triggers the pineal gland to convert sleep-enhancing (melatonin) hormones to those that increase alertness (serotonin). Similarly, moderate exposure to sunlight has been found to effectively regulate these hormones and will help you get a better night's rest!

Multiple Sclerosis: How sunlight makes a difference!

Multiple Sclerosis (MS) is an extremely debilitating disease, and it is now thought that low levels of vitamin D can promote its onset. Likewise, research has shown that the severity of the disease can be decreased by sun exposure and vitamin D. Numerous studies have also found that the risk of death related to MS is significantly reduced by moderate sunlight exposure, with some reporting as high as a 76 percent reduction in early mortality risk.

Amazing Health Facts

According to new research, adults who don't get enough of the "sunshine vitamin" are 26 percent more likely to die early.

Supplementing your vitamin D with a pill is not the best way to receive adequate amounts of this essential vitamin. Because vitamin D is fat-soluble, excess amounts are stored in the body for later use and can lead to a condition known as hypercalcaemia, which is too much calcium in the blood. Symptoms of hypercalcaemia can include fatigue, depression, confusion, nausea, and constipation. For safely obtaining adequate amounts of vitamin D, moderate exposure to sunlight is still your best option.

Cow's milk is actually a poor source of vitamin D. One quart of untreated milk contains roughly 50 to 80 IUs of vitamin D. This is why the dairy industry has been adding vitamin D to milk at a rate of 400 IUs per quart since the 1930s. Oddly, research has shown that the vitamin D in enriched milk is not easily absorbed by the body.

Amazing Health Fact

Get the right light at the right time. Researchers have found that sleeping for several hours in nighttime darkness promotes a healthy blood level of melatonin, which can significantly suppress the growth and proliferation of breast tumors. They also found that sleeping while exposed to light at night causes a dramatic drop in blood melatonin levels, setting the stage for growth and proliferation of breast cancer cells.

Mental Health and Fatigue: Can sunlight help you think better?

When the body's hormones are functioning optimally, sunlight causes the production of melatonin to decrease and serotonin to increase. Not only is serotonin the chemical the brain uses to produce alertness, it also helps create a feeling of happiness. That's why experts recommend waking up early — so you can take full advantage of a day's worth of natural light!

The Best Light in the World!

"God is light, and in him is no darkness at all" (1 John 1:5).

We have seen that sunlight is essential to good health. However, could another type of light be essential for our spiritual well-being?

The Bible says that Jesus created the physical world: "He was in the beginning with God. All things were made through Him" (John 1:2, 3 NKJV). And in the Creation account itself, it was the Word of God that first provided light to the world — because the sun, moon, and stars were created on the fourth day.

Interestingly, Christ is also referred to as the "Word" (John 1:14). It is no coincidence then that He says, "I am the light of the world" (John 9:5 NKJV).

Scientists believe that someday the sun will burn out. However, Jesus desires to give us light now beyond that which is seen. He says, "I am the light of the world. He who follows Me shall not walk in darkness, but have the light of life" (John 8:12 NKJV).

Just as sunlight has powerful healing potential for our bodies, Jesus, the Light of the world, is the best healing sunshine for our souls. "To you who fear My name The Sun of Righteousness shall arise with healing in His wings" (Malachi 4:2 NKJV).

Visit our website at **www.AmazingHealthFacts.org** to learn more about the Light of the world, who provides eternal health! ◾

Learn More
about the connection between
Mind, Body, & Spirit

Sign up for a *FREE* Bible study course at
www.AmazingHealthFacts.org

Discover what the Bible really says about:

- Healthy living
- Life after death
- Heaven and hell
- Happier marriage
- Lasting peace
- And more!

Temperance

(moderation)

In the beginning …
the choice was clear.

> *"The LORD God commanded the man, saying, 'Of every tree of the garden you may freely eat; but of the tree of the knowledge of good and evil you shall not eat, for in the day that you eat of it you shall surely die' " (Genesis 2:16, 17 NKJV).*

Few marine animals are as mysterious, hypnotic, and intimidating as jellyfish. These bizarre gelatinous creatures are 97 percent water and quite transparent, hence the name "jellyfish."

At first glance, it's amazing that they are living at all. They have no heart, no blood, and no gills, bones, or cartilage. Scientists have determined that some jellies have eyes that can detect light, which is amazing when you consider that they don't have a brain!

Jellyfish move up and down by using special muscles to draw water into the bell and then push it out again, yet they really have no choice where they are going. They are basically carried about whichever way the wind and water currents move them.

But unlike the jellyfish, God gave man a brain and the power of choice.

Does God really mean what He says?

In the beginning, God gave Adam and Eve freedom to eat from the tree of life and almost every other fruit in the garden. But He warned that eating — or even touching — the forbidden fruit of one tree would result in death. The tree of the knowledge of good and evil stood in the midst of the garden as a choice between loyalty or disobedience. Sadly, these first humans ended up viewing this dangerous fruit as good for food and for enhancing their wisdom.

They went against God's clear command and, in one bite, a tsunami of sin and heartache swept across this world. And even though this forbidden tree is no longer in this world, could there be other "forbidden fruits" today that sap our joy and rob us of our freedom?

Amazing Health Fact

According to the Bible, sin entered through man's choice. Indeed, the Bible's definition of sin is the breaking of God's laws (1 John 3:4). It wasn't merely because man ate a piece of fruit — it was a decision to rebel against the goodness of His wisdom and instruction.

Amazing Physiology

The Frontal Lobe

In September 1848, a 25-year-old railroad foreman, Phineas P. Gage, was using an iron rod to pack explosive powder into a hole when a powerful blast propelled the 13-pound tamping iron like a bullet through his head. Amazingly, this traumatic accident did not kill Phineas. In fact, he regained his physical strength and lived for another 13 years. He also seemed mentally sound — he could speak and do physical tasks just as well as before, and his memory seemed unimpaired.

Yet friends and family knew he was no longer the same man. Before the accident, he was a well-loved, responsible worker and husband. He was known by all as a pious and dependable man. But after the accident, Phineas experienced a major moral decline. He became very short tempered, rude, and foul mouthed. He started to smoke and drink and lost all respect for spiritual things. It seemed as though his ethical filters had been turned off.

Phineas' accident ended up costing him his moral standards and his commitment to loved ones. Researchers have concluded that he had lost a very important part of his brain called the "frontal lobe," a section of the brain that is responsible for moral reasoning, judgment, social behavior, and spirituality. Amazingly, the Bible even talks about a "mark" in the forehead that can mean the difference between life and death!

Where are decisions really made?

The frontal lobe of the brain is the key to our rational, moral, and ethical decision making. It is the part of the brain that defines our character, personality, and will. Essentially, the frontal lobe is the section of our brains that contains our spiritual nature. Because of this, Satan is constantly trying to destroy or cloud this part of the brain.

Amazing Health Fact

The term "lobotomy" refers to a surgical operation that destroys the function of the frontal lobe. During the early 1900s, this procedure was extremely popular in treating mental illnesses such as schizophrenia, extreme depression, and psychotic disorders. It was even reportedly used in cases of childhood disobedience! However, this irreversible procedure robbed people of their individuality and freedom of rational thought.

What happens when the frontal lobe malfunctions?

Experts have linked frontal lobe damage with schizophrenia, bipolar disorder, obsessive-compulsive disorder, depression, and numerous other mental illnesses. Some of the effects of frontal lobe damage can include:

- impairment of moral principle,
- social impairment,
- lack of foresight,
- loss of abstract reasoning,
- diminished ability for math,
- lack of restraint (boasting, hostility, aggressiveness),
- memory impairment (especially of recent events),
- distractibility and restlessness,
- emotional instability,
- apathy (lack of initiative),
- and indifference to one's condition (happy-go-lucky).

What are common causes of frontal lobe damage?

Traumatic events, such as car accidents, account for some of the most severe forms of frontal lobe damage. However, amazingly, the most common form of frontal lobe damage comes from unhealthy lifestyle choices.

For example, one study discovered that obese women with high levels of C-reactive protein have corresponding frontal lobe impairments. This protein is associated with inflammation and is strongly linked to a sedentary lifestyle.

The frontal lobe is also very sensitive to the effects of toxic chemicals. For instance, alcohol, drugs, caffeine, and tobacco have all been found to damage the frontal lobe.

The Evidence

Research proves that modern "forbidden fruits" impair health and longevity.

What is the definition of a "forbidden fruit"?

In Genesis 3:1–6, some key factors characterized the infamous forbidden fruit:

1. Eating it eventually caused death.
2. It had pleasurable qualities. (But not everything that's pleasant is forbidden!)
3. It affected the frontal lobe. (Thoughts of shame originate in the frontal lobe.)

Keeping these factors in mind, let's take a look at some potential modern-day "forbidden fruits."

Special Report: Alcohol

The Unquenchable Thirst?

Does alcohol impair decision making?

Alcohol use is responsible for millions of cases of disabling mental illness each year. Often overlooked, one factor affects 100 percent of alcohol users: frontal lobe impairment.

The neurotransmitter responsible for halting an action or nerve impulse in the brain is known as "gamma-aminobutyric acid" (GABA). Alcohol blocks the action of GABA at the nerve junction, enabling you to do things your conscience wouldn't normally allow. This results in an increase of risky behaviors, aggression, and impulsivity. Eventually, these actions might even become habitual. The

more times a neuron carries out an impulse, the more likely it is to allow the same action.

The results can be lethal: One study revealed that alcohol intoxication increases the risk of suicide by 90 times! Worse yet, alcohol can alter neuron DNA, thereby passing brain damage down from generation to generation.

Many "social drinkers" mistakenly believe that alcohol makes them more confident. Yet confidence has to do with the execution of a task without anxiety. Those who rely on alcohol for certain tasks have never actually built up the confidence through logical decision making. And during acute intoxication, you are more of a passenger than a driver. Bottom line: If you value your ability to make rational decisions, steer completely clear of alcohol!

Government studies show that 1 out of 10 drinkers will become an alcoholic. The Bible says, "Woe to those who rise early in the morning, That they may follow intoxicating drink; Who continue until night, till wine inflames them!" (Isaiah 5:11 NKJV).

Amazing Health Fact

are not the only ones affected — even social drinkers die younger than non-drinkers.

Alcohol is not a harmless social beverage, but rather a mind-altering, addictive drug. It is mistaken to suggest that drinking alcohol is nothing more than a benign personal choice. Alcohol consumption is involved in half of all murders, half of all violent crime, one third of all

But isn't alcohol good for the heart?

According to numerous studies, red wine might reduce the risk of heart disease. However, other studies show that alcohol is toxic to the heart muscle. How, then, does red wine reduce heart disease risk? The red grape! The skin of red grapes contains high levels of chemicals known as "flavonoids," which have been found to have health-promoting effects. In fact, the flavonoid quercetin is an extremely powerful antioxidant that has been shown to reduce heart disease risk. Thus, the heart-protective effects from "moderate" consumption of red wine come from the grape skin and not the alcohol. Indeed, studies have shown that red grape juice has exactly the same heart benefits without the toxic side effects of the alcohol.

Amazing Health Fact

In a 2001 survey, almost half of Americans aged 12 or older reported being current drinkers of alcohol — an estimated 109 million people.

child abuse, one third of all suicides, more than half of all domestic violence incidents, half of all traffic deaths, and a large portion of unwanted pregnancies, sexual assaults, and divorces! It is the world's most destructive drug and costs U.S. taxpayers nearly $200 billion a year!

Isn't moderate alcohol use good for health?

Alcohol is responsible for up to 30 percent of the worldwide incidence of esophageal cancer, liver cancer, liver cirrhosis, epileptic conditions, automobile accidents, and homicides. In fact, alcohol consumption is a likely cause of more than 60 different types of diseases and disabilities. It is estimated that alcohol use results in 1.8 million deaths annually worldwide. And heavy drinkers

Amazing Health Fact

What is temperance? One writer put it simply as "the complete abstinence from that which is harmful, and the moderate use of that which is good." You don't have to deny yourself everything that is pleasing, but it is important to moderate all that you do.

when new drugs are used, they create an even more intense pleasure response, leading to stronger future addictions.

Chemicals released in this runaway pleasure response, such as the protein dynorphin, actually depress the entire pleasure response system. Thus, ordinary pleasurable experiences lose their appeal. Addictive drugs become the pleasure of choice, an all consuming desire. Due to genetic damage, children can inherit heightened sensitivity to addictive drugs. If you have great-grandparents, grandparents, or parents who abused alcohol, tobacco, or any other kind of addictive drug, you are at much greater risk for forming strong addictions.

Special Report: Drugs

Heaven on Earth?

How do people get addicted?

Did you know that your brain is naturally wired for pleasure? This isn't a bad thing, because the pleasure circuit of the brain can help reinforce healthy behavior, such as exercising, reading, productive hobbies, etc.

However, certain substances can take over this natural process and lead to addiction. Addiction is characterized by two distinct processes: tolerance and dependence.

- **TOLERANCE** means that the brain becomes accustomed to the pleasurable stimulation and demands increasing levels to achieve the same response.

- **DEPENDENCE** describes the adverse emotional and physical reactions that occur after the pleasing stimulation is removed.

Research has shown that illicit drugs, such as cocaine, and even many "legal" drugs can cause permanent structural changes in both brain cells and genetic material. Using an addictive drug can actually alter the brain cells to become more sensitive to other addictive substances. Thus,

What are some other deadly legal drugs?

Illegal drugs — such as heroin, cocaine, methamphetamines, etc. — have caused much disease and death in America. However, you might be surprised to learn that prescription drugs kill far more people every year than illegal drugs. In fact, one study showed that the fourth leading cause of death in America is the side effects of properly prescribed medication! Although many prescription drugs can alleviate symptoms and help regulate bodily processes, they can be toxic to another bodily system or organ. (Note: See your doctor before you stop taking prescribed medicine!)

Amazing Health Fact

Researchers have demonstrated that the choices we make and the actions we take actually result in physical changes in the brain. For cocaine users, dormant genes causing the production of proteins that produce cravings for more cocaine are turned on.

Amazing Health Fact

Nearly half (46 percent) of the 55,000 cases for primary prescription drug abuse in 2008 were for prescription pain-relieving narcotic drugs like Demerol.

For example, acetaminophen, taken by millions of Americans each year to relieve pain or bring down a high body temperature, can, if used unwisely, result in extensive liver damage. In fact, the overdose of acetaminophen is the leading cause of liver failure in America. Each year, more than 56,000 emergency room visits are attributable to overdose of this drug. Even at recommended doses, acetaminophen can cause liver damage and the routine use of this drug almost doubles the risk of developing kidney cancer.

Amazing Health Fact

It is generally true that anything you can become addicted to, from heroin to caffeine, is bad for your health. Nobody has ever become addicted to bananas or broccoli.

Unlike illicit drugs and some medications used unwisely, healthy lifestyle choices bring pleasure and healing … all without side effects!

NOTICE: Do not stop or otherwise make changes to your current medication regimen without first consulting with your doctor!

Special Report: Caffeine

The Real Energy Boost?

Can caffeine affect your judgment?

Since caffeine binds itself to receptors that inhibit certain impulses, the activity of stimulating neurotransmitters is increased. This neurotransmitter imbalance can lead to mental illnesses caused by an increased amount of the neurotransmitter dopamine.

Is caffeine addictive?

Caffeine has been shown to satisfy all the criteria for the second phase of addiction — dependence. In fact, caffeine is the most widely used dependence-creating substance in the world! Caffeine withdrawal can produce headaches, fatigue, irritability, and other adverse physical and mental symptoms.

And when caffeine is combined with a dopamine-stimulating substance or event, the result can be addictive! Sugar, fat, carbonation, intense flavors and aromas, and pleasing sights and sounds all have the potential to trigger the release of significant amounts of dopamine. Coffee, especially "specialty coffee," often contains large amounts of sugar, fat, and appealing flavors and aroma — turning the occasional drinker into an addicted repeat customer!

Amazing Health Fact

The white, bitter-tasting, crystalline substance known as caffeine was first isolated from coffee in 1820. Today, caffeine is the world's most popular drug.

Is caffeine robbing your sleep?

Caffeine comes from a family of chemicals called methylxanthines. In high doses, caffeine is lethal to humans. In low doses, it can reduce fatigue, improve circulation, and many other stimulating effects. However, this extra stimulation comes at a high cost.

The term "homeostasis" describes the body's attempt to maintain balance and health. Naturally, periods of stimulation should be accompanied with periods of adequate rest. In fact, the body has several defense mechanisms to help

Amazing Health Facts

Heavy soda or coffee drinkers that stop drinking caffeine normally experience a headache, and sometimes nausea. Fortunately, caffeine withdrawal occurs in five days or less with most people. As you are stopping, make sure to eat a good diet, get adequate rest, and exercise.

"Decaffeinated" coffee is not totally caffeine free, containing about 3 milligrams of caffeine.

Coffee is the world's most popular stimulant drink: 4 out of 5 Americans drink it, consuming more than 400 million cups a day. But women who drink just two or more cups of coffee a day have an increased risk of developing osteoporosis.

One study found that young people who consumed more than five caffeinated beverages a day had almost twice the odds of developing a hemorrhagic stroke. The same study found that adults who took higher amounts of caffeine (in the form of caffeine-containing drugs) had almost four times the odds for a hemorrhagic stroke! (Hemorrhagic stroke occurs in almost 60,000 Americans every year and has a 50 percent mortality rate.)

maintain an optimal balance between stimulation and rest.

However, caffeine removes these defense mechanisms and allows the body to continue in a state of increased stimulation — even while sleeping! Studies have shown that as little as 200 mg of caffeine in the morning can impact sleep the following evening. Caffeine especially affects the deeper stages of sleep, when the brain is normally in a state of decreased activity.

Is caffeine really that much of a headache?

Both routine caffeine use and withdrawal can trigger headaches, which is partly why it causes dependence. Surprisingly, caffeine is one of the active ingredients in many pain relievers; thus, you might be causing future headaches while trying to prevent them!

Caffeine, especially in high doses, increases the amount of adenosine in the brain. High levels of adenosine cause blood vessels to widen excessively, a process that has been linked with aneurysms — defects in the wall of a blood vessel that have the potential to rupture.

Amazing Health Fact

Most energy drinks contain at least as much caffeine as an 8-ounce cup of coffee: 80mg!

Adding to that health danger are excessive amounts of sugar and suspect herbal stimulants.

Special Report: Tobacco

Hiding Behind a Smokescreen?

Was tobacco ever healthy?

Although much is known today about the deadly and addictive effects of tobacco, years ago it was thought to be a healthy habit. Doctors even prescribed tobacco for its apparent benefits on mood, physical vigor, ear infections, and even lung disease!

Over time, of course, increasing evidence revealed the health risks of tobacco use. However, tobacco companies still denied that their products were related to death, disease, or addiction. In fact, it took decades for them to admit that cigarettes were harmful and

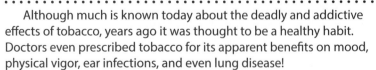

addictive. Moreover, we now know that these companies had ample evidence that their products were dangerous. As a result, tobacco companies were sued and legislation was passed demanding that these companies label their products as addictive and harmful.

Yet surprisingly, many still buy their deadly products!

Why are people still using tobacco?

Tobacco companies realized that anything that can make the normally noxious process of inhaling smoke more pleasurable will also increase the strength of a cigarette addiction.

Cigarette smoke contains at least 600 added ingredients, including sugar, menthol, and ammonia. Sugar is added to enhance the taste and can account for as much as 10 percent of the total weight of the cigarette. Menthol is used to numb nerves that would normally convey a pain response from smoke inhalation. (This additive is especially detrimental to new smokers, as their lungs are especially sensitive to smoke.) Ammonia is used to increase the pH of cigarette smoke, ensuring nicotine absorption to keep the smoker coming back for more.

Do tobacco companies care about health?

Despite being forced to pour millions of dollars into stop-smoking campaigns, tobacco companies continue to spend millions more each year on advertising and marketing. The bottom line is that if tobacco companies really cared about your health, they would close up shop instead of recruiting new smokers.

Today, we have to make the right choice — we can choose to be a victim or to abstain. See page 43 to learn more about the effects of smoking.

Studies have also shown that certain behaviors, such as gambling, viewing pornography, shopping, and watching TV, can be just as destructive as any chemical dependency.

Amazing Health Fact

You can choose a better tree!

"The tree of life was also in the midst of the garden" (Genesis 2:9 NKJV).

In addition to the forbidden tree in Eden, there was another important tree — the tree of life, which had the power to provide eternal vitality to humanity.

Just as the two trees provided a choice for Adam and Eve in the garden, a similar choice is offered to everyone today. We can choose true wisdom and life — or we can choose deception, addiction, and death.

When God offered His Son as a sacrifice on the cross, He provided the only antidote for the most deadly addiction of all time: the addiction of sin. The cross became a new tree of life and Jesus' perfect life the only healing fruit. Jesus said, "Whoever eats My flesh and drinks My blood has eternal life" (John 6:54 NKJV). This means accepting His sacrifice for your sins, reading His Word, and believing His message of forgiveness and power.

Satan has been working hard to blind people to this "tree of life." And he wants to attack your frontal lobe because it gives you the rational power to see past his deceptions!

Unfortunately, many have allowed their brains to become so clouded by bad habits that they are unable to clearly see the truth. But God promises you something real, something you can trust. In the end … the decision is still clear … but this time the decision is yours. Make it with a clear mind! Reach out for the fruit of life and accept God's promises today! To learn more, visit **www.AmazingHealthFacts.org.** ■

Tree of Life

Air

In the beginning …
breath gave life.

> *"The LORD God formed man of the dust of the ground, and breathed into his nostrils the breath of life; and man became a living being" (Genesis 2:7 NKJV).*

In the last century, man has conquered some of the most extreme environments — exploring the deepest oceans, scaling the highest mountains, and even venturing into outer space. But one common challenge had to be overcome before any of these achievements were possible: The adventurers had to learn how to take their air with them so they could breathe.

Breathed Into Being

Looking closely at the biblical creation account, you'll notice something very unique in how God created mankind. He formed Adam with His own hands and breathed His "breath of life" into his lungs. If the "breath of life" began our existence, it stands to reason the absence of that breath can terminate it.

As you'll see, the air you breathe and how well you breathe it has a huge impact on how long you actually remain a living being: It can either be a "savour of life unto life"… or "death unto death" (2 Corinthians 2:16). Take a deep breath … and keep reading!

Amazing Physiology

Why is air such a heavy subject?

Oxygen is our body's most important physical need. Although air is composed of only about 20 percent oxygen, each inhalation brings this life-sustaining gas into the lungs. Oxygen then diffuses into the bloodstream, where it is transported all over the body via your red blood cells. It is mostly used to facilitate reactions involving the body's main energy source: glucose. Without oxygen this energy source would be useless.

A Fire Within

The reaction between glucose and oxygen can be compared to a burning candle. If oxygen levels are decreased enough, a candle will "go out." In the same way, if oxygen levels get too low in your body, your "lights will go out" (lose consciousness). Just like the burning candle, your body also produces smoke as a byproduct of combustion. You cannot see this smoke, but every time you exhale, carbon dioxide and water vapor are released into the air.

How can a negative be a positive?

Health is truly improved by breathing "fresh" air. Have you ever gone for a walk after a thunderstorm or by the sea shore? Do you remember feeling invigorated? It could be because you were breathing in air rich in negative ions, which are naturally found outside where radiation is present (sunlight, forests, mountains, turbulent water, after thunderstorms, etc.).

Is there anything you can do to breathe better?

Fortunately, breathing is innate, but many people have bad breathing habits and don't use their lungs effectively. Ideally, breathing should expand the lungs through lowering the diaphragm (a muscle separating the lungs from the abdominal organs). This can be accomplished by relaxing the abdominal muscles during inhalation. The idea is to expand your upper lung area as well as your lower lung area, resulting in increased lung function,

Amazing Health Fact

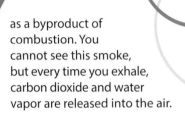

We wouldn't be souls without air. According to the Bible, we become a soul when two elements are present: dust and breath (Genesis 2:7 KJV).

"deeper breathing," and a more efficient oxygen/carbon dioxide exchange. In fact, the practice of deep breathing is one of the simplest ways of preventing certain types of pneumonia.

There's no air like home air … right?

Generally speaking, the quality of outside air is far superior to the air found circulating in your home. In fact, one study suggests that indoor air can be up to five times more polluted than outdoor air — which is bad news when you consider that the average American spends 90 percent of their time indoors. Indeed, this combination of pollution exposure and duration of exposure makes indoor air quality a serious health issue.

One of the major contributors to indoor air pollution is particulate matter (tiny particles suspended in the air). High levels of particulate matter are responsible for a host of medical conditions. The simple remedy for this problem is opening windows and letting fresh air circulate through the house. But remember, short, sporadic breathing is not healthy to you or your house — so allow your home to take deep breaths! In heavily polluted

Amazing Health Fact

Want to "up" the amount of negative ions in your home? Numerous commercial in-home ionizers are on the market. But buyer beware, some have been found to produce ozone and undesirable atmospheric free-radicals. The safest source is nature: Potted plants naturally increase oxygen and levels of negative ions while reducing carbon dioxide.

environments, such as cities, experts recommend airing out your house at night because smog levels fall significantly after sunset.

Are you really affected by outdoor air pollution?

A recent report by the British government revealed that life expectancy was reduced by nearly a year due to air pollution. Fortunately, many local newscasts now offer forecasts for outdoor air quality, such as ground-level ozone and pollen. It is best to limit outdoor activity during periods of high ground-level ozone because breathing this air can result in lung damage.

Unfortunately, outdoor air in large metropolitan areas has been found to have increased concentrations of ground-level ozone, positive ions, smog, carbon dioxide, and other contaminants. This is because cities have more automobiles and factories, while having less vegetation to eliminate toxins and convert carbon dioxide to oxygen. Moreover, the friction of air flowing against manmade structures (skyscrapers) reduces the amount of negative ions in the air. Due to these factors, many cities are, by nature, places of increased anxiety, tension, headaches, and a host of other health problems related to poor air quality.

Amazing Health Fact

Deep breathing can help relieve headaches, backaches, stomachaches, and sleeplessness. It allows blood pressure to return to normal and releases natural mood enhancers (endorphins) into the bloodstream. Use deep breathing ... it's one of the best techniques for stress relief!

Too much of a good thing…

Rapid breathing during exercise is healthy and necessary because the body needs extra amounts of oxygen. However, hyperventilation (abnormally rapid breathing) caused by anxiety and nervousness can lead to an excess of oxygen in the blood and a corresponding decrease in carbon dioxide levels. When this happens, the body's pH balance is disturbed (known as "respiratory alkalosis"). Symptoms include dizziness and rapid heartbeat. A common treatment for hyperventilation is breathing into a paper bag, which restores normal carbon dioxide levels.

Amazing Health Facts

The right lung has three separate compartments, while the left lung has only two.

The average person takes 21,600 breaths per day, using about 88 pounds of oxygen. Our brain uses 25 percent of all the oxygen we take in.

The Evidence

Research proves the connection between breathing air, health, and longevity.

Cardiovascular Disease: Is air quality related to heart disease?

A recent study conducted in Italy found that the incidence of blood clots was higher among people exposed to increased levels of particulate matter. This translates into an increased risk of death from pulmonary embolism, stroke, and even heart attack.

Another study found that reducing the amount of indoor air pollution through HEPA filtration improved microvascular blood flow by an average of 8 percent. Improved microvascular blood flow can help in the treatment of such conditions as angina and diabetic circulatory complications. Plus, one study found up to a 30 percent increase in mortality among those with heart disease who lived closest to areas of increased pollution (highways, bus routes, etc.).

Can polluted air affect cholesterol?

The ultra-fine particles found in smog actually decrease levels of HDL, the good cholesterol. In one study, mice exposed to these microscopic particles had a 55 percent increase in atherosclerotic plaque development (hardening of the arteries). Mice exposed to larger pollution particles only had a 25 percent increase. Researchers also point out that these microscopic particles are so small they cannot be captured by air filtration!

Amazing Health Fact

Sleep apnea is a disorder characterized by a pause or cessation of rhythmic breathing during sleep. This condition interrupts restful sleep and is much more common among overweight adults. Apnea sufferers have a 30 percent higher risk of heart attack or premature death than those unaffected. Put simply, losing extra weight will also help you breathe a lot more easily.

Cancer: Smoking causes cancer, but can polluted air do the same?

Worldwide, indoor air pollution is thought to cause more than 1.5 percent of the approximately 1 million lung cancer deaths per year.

It is also estimated that radon gas affects one out of every 15 homes in America. Why is this important? The American Lung Association rates radon as the second-leading cause of lung cancer in the United States — up to

Amazing Health Fact

Worldwide, 1.4 billion people breathe polluted air. That's sad when considering that on average, air pollution takes a year off the typical human lifespan. In California alone, up to 17,000 premature deaths each year are due to particulate air pollution.

20,000 lung cancer deaths per year, second only to smoking.

Radon test kits are widely available and inexpensive, but the single most effective way of increasing the quality of indoor air is proper ventilation. Other indoor contaminates such as formaldehyde (found in pressed-wood products, paneling, etc.) are estimated to contribute about 6,500 additional lung cancer deaths each year.

Mental Health: How does air affect your brain?

Keeping brain cells healthy is vital to combating mental health issues such as depression and anxiety, while improving overall mental performance. For this, the brain needs an almost constant supply of oxygen. If you are not

Amazing Health Fact

Winds that blow in certain areas of the world are naturally full of positive ions, including the Santa Ana winds in California and the Sharar winds in Israel and Egypt. During the time these winds blow, many people develop problems with increased anxiety and suspicion, headaches, irritability, respiratory problems, etc. In fact, courts in some countries actually pronounce lighter sentences for crimes committed during the time of these winds.

after leaving the building. And again, the problem is best alleviated through adequate ventilation!

Numerous other particles found in indoor air, such as mold spores, dust mites, and even airborne bacteria can cause respiratory irritation and illness. Indeed, indoor air has significantly more circulating bacteria and fungi than outdoor air. Some researchers have even identified mold spores as the cause in most chronic sinus infections affecting 37 million Americans each year.

Can breathing bad air actually cause asthma?

Breathing air contaminated by household chemical compounds (cleaners, polishes, etc.) might lead to the onset of asthma. Researchers found that young children exposed to higher levels of these chemicals were significantly more likely to develop respiratory problems, such as asthma, later on in life.

Amazing Health Fact

Does it seem like your children are always sick? Do they have trouble concentrating in school? Well, studies have shown that 1 in 5 of the nation's schools have unsatisfactory indoor air quality. Furthermore, 1 in 4 schools were designated as having poor ventilation. Meanwhile, rates of childhood asthma and attention disorders continue to rise.

adequately oxygenated, the brain will be the first to suffer. (Fainting is actually a defense mechanism to protect the brain from low oxygen levels.)

Asthma/Allergies: What makes a building "sick"?

Millions of American office workers are exposed to poor-quality indoor air. While at their jobsites, many workers develop fatigue, sore throats, difficulty in concentration, and other allergy-like symptoms. These sicknesses are collectively known as "sick building syndrome." The key to diagnose this is whether or not the symptoms quickly disappear

Lung disease/ illnesses: **WHO** cares about bad air?

The World Health Organization (WHO) estimates that, globally, almost 700,000 of the 2.7 million deaths from lung disease per year are caused by indoor air pollution. The WHO also estimates that exposure to indoor air pollution almost doubles the risk of pneumonia. In fact, indoor air pollution is estimated to cause more than 900,000 of the 2 million yearly pneumonia-related deaths worldwide.

Amazing Health Fact

Motor vehicles produce more air pollution than any other single human activity.

Special Report: Smoking

With all the bad press, why hasn't smoking become less popular?

The U.S. Center for Disease Control has labeled smoking as the single most preventable cause of premature death in America, claiming the lives of more than 400,000 annually. Smoking is believed to cut off, on average, 21 years of life.

Globally, the death toll is worse, claiming the lives of more than one out of three men age 35 to 69. The WHO estimates that smoking causes over 3 million deaths per year. If current rates of smoking continue, by the year 2030, the yearly death toll will be more than 10 million.

Amazing Health Fact

Not Just Humans — the health effects of smog have been seen in dolphins living off the coasts of large cities. In a recent study, dolphins showed signs of black lung, an illness usually found among coal miners.

What's in cigarette smoke anyway?

Smoking not only causes cancer but numerous other diseases due to harmful chemicals found in cigarette smoke. Indeed, cigarette smoke contains more than 4,000 different chemicals, and many of these are known to cause cancer:

- formaldehyde, which is commonly used to preserve dead bodies,
- arsenic, which is used to kill rats,
- ammonia, which is used to clean toilets,
- acetone, which is used to remove nail polish,
- carbon monoxide, which also comes out of your car's exhaust pipe,
- and hydrogen cyanide, a poison used to execute people in gas chambers.

Tried to quit but can't break the habit?

Did you know that smoking also affects mental health? Nicotine has been found to excessively increase serotonin levels, which causes anxiety. Perhaps this is one

of the reasons researchers have linked the daily quantity of cigarettes smoked and an increase in anxiety disorders. When a person stops smoking, serotonin levels drop — a process that might lead to depression.

Unfortunately, nicotine withdrawal can also cause anxiety. Indeed, quitting smoking can temporarily make you totally miserable. This is part of the reason many can't seem to quit. Don't despair! There are many things you can do to bring your emotions back into balance.

What are some tips to prevent depression after you stop smoking?

The Weimar Center of Health & Education suggests the following steps to help improve mood and combat depression:

1) Eat a plant-based diet, which helps to raise serotonin levels.
2) Maximize serotonin levels by eating soy beans, pumpkin seeds, sesame seeds, almonds, and beans.
3) Get 30 minutes of exposure to bright sunlight in the morning or take two 15-minute walks outdoors between 9:00 AM and 3:00 PM daily.
4) Walk briskly for one hour, six days a week.
5) Eat two or three tablespoons of freshly ground flaxseed daily.
6) Eat between one-fourth and half a cup of English walnuts at breakfast and lunch.
7) Take a B-complex vitamin with your noon or evening meal.
8) Dismiss negative thoughts and speak nothing negative of others.

If you want to quit smoking, will it be easier if you taper off?

If you truly desire to quit smoking, the easiest way is to just quit. Studies have shown that those who attempt to "taper off" cigarettes have more prolonged nicotine withdrawal symptoms than those who quit "cold turkey."

Make the decision today to stop smoking: Studies have shown that almost as soon as you quit, the body starts to heal. And after just a few years, the risk of related diseases, such as lung cancer, actually approaches the same risks faced by nonsmokers!

The Breath of Life

The emotional pain and turmoil caused by quitting smoking has been compared to the loss of a friend. But you don't have to despair. You can start building a healthier friendship today with someone who has been waiting to fill that very void in your life and in your lungs.

"Thus says God the LORD, Who created the heavens and stretched them out, Who spread forth the earth and that which comes from it, Who gives breath to the people on

it, And spirit to those who walk on it" (Isaiah 42:5 NKJV).

For mankind, the spark of life was God's exhalation — His Word breathed into a man. "When he had said this, [Jesus] breathed on them, and saith unto them, Receive ye the Holy Ghost" (John 20:22).

Whether we realize it or not, we are all longing for something more than just optimal respiration. We were formed by a unique act for a very unique relationship. "He gives to all life, breath, and all things" (Acts 17:25 NKJV).

Why not take time today to see how this incredible relationship can bring a breath of fresh air into your life? Visit **www.AmazingHealthFacts.org!** ■

Resources for a
HEALTHIER, FULLER LIFE!

A Better Way of Life
Enjoy more than 120 healthy, easy-to-make recipes along with cooking tips to save you time and effort. Includes an insider's guide to the what, where, and how of plant-based eating, nutrition, and calorie information for weight loss—plus, inspirational tidbits to encourage you on your path to better health!
BK-ABWOL ... $24.98

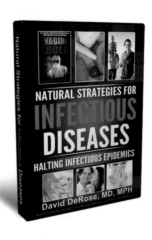

Natural Strategies for Infectious Diseases DVD
Infectious diseases are a serious threat to human health—the flu, tuberculosis, and coronavirus, just to name a few. But you can increase your body's ability to ward off and heal from these diseases! These presentations by expert Dr. David DeRose will give you peace of mind and practical knowledge to empower your body's natural defenses.
DV-ID ... $19.98

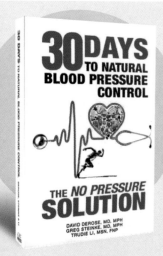

30 Days to Natural Blood Pressure Control
Health expert Dr. David DeRose uncovers the powerful, natural wellness strategies that have helped tens of thousands decrease or even eliminate their need for blood pressure medications. If you are looking for inexpensive, natural ways to control your blood pressure, this book will change your life!
BK-NBPC ... $19.98

Diabetes Undone Set
Presented by diabetes experts Dr. Wes Youngberg and Brenda Davis, this all-in-one set will empower you through a hope-filled journey to reverse diabetes and reclaim your health! Find the root causes of high blood sugar, take advantage of comprehensive health testing, and much more.
DV-DUSET ... $95.98

Find these resources and more at

AFBOOKSTORE.COM

Rest

In the beginning …
God created sleep.

"The Lord God caused a deep sleep to fall on Adam, and he slept; and He took one of his ribs, and closed up the flesh in its place. Then the rib which the Lord God had taken from man He made into a woman, and He brought her to the man" (Genesis 2:21, 22 NKJV).

Did you know that just one hour of sleep deprivation increases the number of highway accidents by eight percent — but that an hour of extra sleep decreases them by eight percent? It's true! It happens every year when daylight saving time changes.

This is because driving effectiveness after you've been awake for 18 hours is about the same as driving after you have had two alcoholic drinks. (One drink = 5 ounces of wine.) When you have been awake for 24 hours, your driving effectiveness is the equivalent of driving under the influence of four to six drinks! Optimum performance comes with eight hours of restful sleep.

We find that the first reference to sleep in the Bible is of a deep and creative sleep. When Adam awoke, he was refreshed, revived … and married. A whole new life and, ultimately, the future of humanity can be traced back to that first nap.

The reality was that even in a perfect world, God designed that a person would need to rest and that night was the optimum time to sleep. "He came to a certain place and stayed there all night, because the sun had set. … And he lay down in that place to sleep" (Genesis 28:11 NKJV).

Could it be that we need to be reminded of the importance of restful sleep, especially in this imperfect, always-on-the-go world?

Amazing Health Fact

A new baby sleeps as much as 16 hours a day. But that same baby could cause up to 700 hours of lost sleep for the parents in the first year!

Amazing Physiology

What's the trouble with troubled sleep?

An estimated 60 million Americans have trouble sleeping. Today, because of artificial lights, TV, the internet, and the caffeine craze, people are sleeping about one hour less than their great-grandparents did. This figure might not be startling in itself — but considering that proper sleep is one of the most important elements in the process of healing, America is also in for a disease-ridden wake-up call.

Sleep is an activity.

Sleep is much more than just a passive experience for your body. Although we might be resting, our body is engaged in another type of activity, a process that will bring restoration and healing to frazzled organs, nerves, and body tissues.

Sleep is characterized by a cycle of five increasingly deeper stages of sleep followed by periods of increased brain activity:

Stage 1: If you have ever driven a car while drowsy, you are well acquainted with this stage of very light sleep. The startle that often awakes drowsy drivers is an indication of having briefly entered this stage.

Stages 2, 3, and 4: In these stages, brain activity decreases (but does not stop); deep sleep begins and delta waves begin and intensify.

Stage 5: This sleep is characterized by rapid eye movement (REM), dreaming, arm and leg paralysis (so we don't act out our dreams), and increased heart rate and blood pressure. The brainwave pattern during REM is close to that of being awake.
It is theorized that REM is a period of information processing, storing, and the improvement of brain efficiency.

What role does melatonin play in sleep?

Melatonin is a hormone produced by the pineal gland in response to darkness. One of the most notable functions of this hormone is its antioxidant capabilities, providing protection from dangerous free radicals inside the cell. This helps to prevent damage to the cell's most vital component: DNA. Damage to DNA has been linked to a host of diseases, such as cancer.

Seven simple steps to a restful night's sleep:

1. Wake up with the sun: Sunlight helps to increase levels of alertness, enhancing hormones such as serotonin.

2. Eat a balanced diet rich in plant-based complex carbohydrates and tryptophan: Foods rich in tryptophan are good not only for sleep, but also for optimal daytime performance. Tryptophan, an amino acid, is necessary for the construction of numerous hormones, including serotonin and melatonin. Carbohydrates help tryptophan enter the brain. Tryptophan-rich foods include: tofu,

Amazing Health Fact

The hormone adenosine induces relaxation to help us sleep, but caffeine blocks the communication between adenosine and the brain, keeping you "awake" and shutting off the body's defense against exhaustion-related injury.

pumpkin seeds, gluten flour, sesame seeds, almonds, black walnuts, and black-eyed cowpeas.

3. Find time for moderate physical exercise: Exercise helps increase levels of certain hormones that have been found to enhance sleep at night.

4. Avoid sleep-depriving substances (alcohol, caffeine, nicotine, etc.): Alcohol robs the body of deep sleep, while caffeine interferes with sleep due to its stimulating properties. Tobacco users miss out on deeper sleep due to nicotine withdrawal during the night. Antidepressants and even sleeping pills can also decrease levels of REM sleep.

5. Have an established, early bedtime: Experts recommend going to sleep at least two-and-a-half hours before midnight. A regular pattern of sleep is also important, even if you sleep during the day. Studies have found that nightshift workers function better with an established sleep/wake cycle.

6. Sleep in the dark: To optimize melatonin, it is important to sleep in total darkness: Exposure to bright light, even for a few moments, can lower melatonin levels.

7. Leave your worries behind: Studies show that emotional stress can cause poor-quality sleep. Those who pray and commit their troubles to God at night sleep better. "I will both lay me down in peace, and sleep: for thou, LORD, only makest me dwell in safety" (Psalm 4:8).

Too much of a good thing …

Although individual sleep requirements can vary, excessive sleep can be detrimental to health. Studies have shown that among adults, sleeping more than 9 hours per day increases the risk of many common diseases, as compared to a more healthful 7 to 8 hours per day.

The Evidence

Research also proves the connection between rest, health, and longevity.

Cardiovascular Disease: Does proper rest contribute to your heart health?

In a study of American nurses, sleep duration was shown to have a significant impact on heart disease. Compared to those sleeping about 8 hours a night, those sleeping less than 5 had a 39 percent greater risk of developing heart disease. Those sleeping 6 hours had an 18 percent increase. Women who slept over 9 hours increased their risk by 37 percent and

Amazing Health Fact

Eating a large meal before bedtime can result in poor-quality sleep. One study found that participants who consumed a large, high-fat meal for dinner had decreased REM sleep and more nighttime awakenings. Eat dinner early and let it be the lightest meal of your day!

increased their risk of heart attack by 45 percent. Another study found that participants who slept less than 6.5 hours a night had 50 percent higher levels of insulin compared to those who slept between 7.5 and 8.5 hours per night. High insulin levels can result in weight gain, high blood pressure, and increased cholesterol — all three contribute to cardiovascular disease!

Cancer: Can your cancer risk be increased due to lack of sleep?

One major factor in cancer is the health of the immune system. A poorly functioning immune system is more prone to overlook precancerous cells, giving them the chance to multiply. Studies show that a decrease in sleep duration does, in fact, impair immune function. Some evidence suggests that losing as much as 3 hours of sleep can decrease immune function by 50 percent!

Diabetes: How does proper sleep affect your risk for diabetes?

An additional study found that sleeping 9 or more hours a night increased the risk of developing diabetes by 29 percent. Those sleeping under 5 hours had an increased risk of 32 percent. The study also pointed out that those sleeping less than 5 hours had significantly higher levels of chronic disease and both the under- and over-sleepers had increased body weight.

Plus, in a German study, those who had difficulty maintaining sleep had significantly higher rates of diabetes. The study, conducted over a period of 10 years, found that men who had troubled sleep patterns had a 60 percent increased risk of developing diabetes. For women, the results were even more shocking: 98 percent!

Amazing Health Fact

Sending your kids to bed early is no longer a "because I said so" event. According to one study, school-age children who had less than nine hours of sleep had dramatically higher rates of obesity and increased temperament issues. And those going to bed after 9 PM were the most at risk for developing these complications!

Obesity: Can too little sleep put on the pounds?

Inadequate sleep has a profound effect on the risk for obesity. In a study of American women, compared to those who slept 7 hours a night, women who slept less than 5 hours had a much greater risk of weight gain and obesity — up to 58 percent! The study concluded that those sleeping 7 to 8 hours per night had the lowest risk for major weight gain.

Indeed, researchers have found a relationship between the body's appetite control hormones and sleep duration. In one study, those sleeping less than 5 hours a night had lower levels of leptin, an appetite-suppressing hormone. To make matters worse, they were also found to have increased levels of a hormone that stimulates the appetite — a total of a 30 percent increase in hunger-promoting hormone levels!

Mental Health: Does sleep affect my brain?

Increased anxiety, confusion, and even mental illness have been attributed to inadequate sleep. One study that looked at the sleeping patterns of nearly 8,000 people during the course of a year found that inadequate sleep significantly increased the risk of depression. The study also found that over-sleeping significantly increased the odds of mental illness.

Amazing Health Fact

The longest documented record for a human going without sleep, without using stimulants, is held by Randy Gardner. In 1964, the 17-year-old student stayed awake for 264 hours ...11 days! Randy reported hallucinations, nausea, paranoia, blurred vision, slurred speech, and memory and concentration lapses.

Special Report: The Rest of the Week

"On the seventh day God ended his work which he had made; and he rested on the seventh day from all his work which he had made. And God blessed the seventh day, and sanctified it: because that in it he had rested from all his work which God created and made" (Genesis 2:2, 3).

Amazing! God actually took time off. But unlike us, God didn't rest because He was tired. Rather, according to the Bible, He reserved and sanctified the 24 hours at the end of the week for spiritual and physical refreshment. The first seventh day must have been very special to God and humanity. It was a way to spend time together, away from the cares of the week. In fact, when God spoke to Moses thousands of years later, He reminded him of the ongoing importance of the seventh day of the week:

*"Remember the Sabbath day, to keep it holy. Six days you shall labor and do all your work, but the seventh day is the Sabbath of the L*ORD *your God. In it you shall do no work: you, nor your son, nor your daughter, nor your manservant, nor your maidservant, nor your cattle, nor your stranger who is within your gates. For in six days the L*ORD *made the heavens and the earth, the sea, and all that is in them, and rested the seventh day. Therefore the L*ORD *blessed the Sabbath day and hallowed it"* *(Exodus 20:8-11 NKJV).*

Of course, the Sabbath involves spiritual rest, but could there be physical benefits from a weekly day of rest too?

Amazing Health Fact

France once changed the weekly cycle to what they thought was a more "logical" decimal-based system, known as the Republican Calendar. New months were invented and a 10-day week was instituted. However, this attempt actually filled up the country's mental institutions and was quickly abandoned.

What's the connection between weekly rest and health?

Seven days make up a week. It surely sounds simple, but the truth is that scientists don't know why the seven-day cycle is so ingrained in cultures around the world. Unlike the years, days, and months, the seven-day week is not based on any solar or lunar pattern. Yet research has shown that we have an internal, biological seven-day cycle — called the circaseptan rhythm. For example, after an organ transplant, the rejection rate is higher for the transplanted organ on the seventh and fourteenth day following operation.

Cardiovascular Health: Can weekly rest improve your heart health?

The preventative and restorative qualities of a weekly day of rest might reduce the risk of heart disease. There are certain risk factors for heart disease that are directly related to mental and physical stress.

One risk factor is increased levels of uric acid in the blood, which can be increased after periods of physical exertion. One study found that the concentration of uric acid in

the blood was increased for up to 21 hours following intense physical activity.

Another risk factor is an increase in the blood levels of fibrinogen, which facilitates the formation of blood clots. Fibrinogen has been found to be increased due to difficult mental problem solving and periods of mental crisis. It has also been found to naturally peak on a seven-day cycle. In one study of more than 5,000 hospitalized male veterans, fibrinogen levels were strangely found to reach a peak on Saturday, Sunday, and Monday.

Two other factors associated with an increased risk of heart disease are stress and high blood pressure. Stress can be physical and mental in nature, both of which can increase blood pressure.

How does a weekly rest day reduce the risk of heart disease?

All of these risk factors are related to stressful mental or physical work. Therefore, the risk for developing heart disease can be lowered through stress reduction.

However, resting from labor does not imply that the Sabbath should be spent in complete inactivity. On the contrary, this kind of behavior can increase your risk of vascular complications. At the same time, studies show that people who keep Saturday as their weekly day of rest show dramatic decreases in the rates of coronary artery disease.

What is the best reason for a weekly day of rest?

After a long week, we all need a little physical "re-creation." Yet far exceeding all other reasons for a weekly Sabbath is that God told us to keep the seventh day holy!

The Bible is full of examples of those who remembered God's fourth commandment, reaping the benefits of both physical and mental rest: Moses, King David, the Apostles, and Jesus Christ!

Before sin we see that there was no need for physical recovery from a draining week of labor. Yet God sanctioned the seventh day anyway as a time of special communion with His creation. Thus the Sabbath rest is most important as a day of optimal spiritual recovery.

Do you have heavy burdens that you carry throughout the week? Are you looking for a rest from guilt, fear, or sorrow? Or are you simply looking for something better in life? There is a way of life that offers hope, happiness, and healing: Jesus said, "Come unto me, all ye that labour and are heavy laden, and I will give you rest" (Matthew 11:28). Would you like to know how you can have better spiritual and physical rest? Visit **www.SabbathTruth.com** to discover more about the seventh-day rest! ■

Trust

The key to a longer, stronger, happier life

"God hath dealt to every man the measure of faith" (Romans 12:3).

A placebo is something that looks like a legitimate drug but is really nothing more than colored water or a starch pill containing no medicinal value at all. These placebos are often given to a patient to reinforce an expectation that their condition will improve. Placebos are also used when testing the effectiveness of new drugs. Research has clearly shown that when patients take a substance that they sincerely believe will heal them, their symptoms often improve or completely disappear.

In fact, in one study doctors successfully eliminated warts by painting them with a brightly colored but inert dye, promising patients the warts would be gone when the color wore off. And in a study of asthmatics, researchers found they could produce dilation of the airways by simply telling people they were inhaling a powerful bronchodilator, even when they weren't. There are thousands of other well-documented examples of how a person's beliefs brought about real physical improvement.

The Faith Factor

This phenomenon might help explain why Jesus frequently said to those He healed, "Your faith has made you well. Go in peace, and be healed of your affliction"

(Mark 5:34 NKJV). Indeed, if a person's faith in doctors and drugs can have such a profound influence on our health, how much more powerful would faith in God be on our physical and spiritual well being?

Jesus said, "If you can believe, all things are possible to him who believes" (Mark 9:23 NKJV). The phenomenal thing about these "faith factor" studies is that when the

Amazing Health Fact

Want to live seven years longer? *Reader's Digest* has reported that in a nationwide study of 21,000 people, those who prayed and attended religious services more than once a week had a seven-year longer life expectancy than those who never attended services.

patients and physicians both believed the patient would get better, healing occurred more frequently. According to one study, "Patients suffering pain after wisdom tooth extraction got just as much relief from a fake application of ultrasound as from a real one, so long as both patient and therapist thought the machine was on." Perhaps this is related to the truth that collective prayer for an individual's healing has demonstrated real results.

Amazing Health Fact

A recent study finds that people who have never married have the highest risk of premature death in the United States. In addition, people who are divorced or separated are 27 percent more likely to die early. Moreover, married men are half as likely to commit suicide as single men, and one third as likely as divorced men. As you can see, social isolation plays a role in mortality.

The Social Factor: Healthy People Need People

"The LORD God said, It is not good that man should be alone" (Genesis 2:18).

From the beginning, God created man to be a social creature. We have been pre-wired with a need for healthy, trusting relationships.

Have you ever looked closely at the Ten Commandments? You'll find the first four deal with our relationship with God, while the final six help us have a trusting relationship with our fellow human beings. This is why Jesus summarized the Decalogue with these two great commandments: to love God and to love our neighbor (Matthew 22:37–40).

Amazingly, modern studies reveal that many health problems can be traced to a breakdown in trust between people. But even more important, trust in God has become increasingly recognized by medicine for its healing influence.

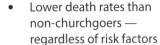

That's why it is so sad that we are now living in a world where divorce is as common as changing tires and lonely people sequester themselves in towering concrete cubicles. The television has become a constant companion, while pithy text messaging has replaced a meaningful visit with neighbors.

Recently, many secular scientists have come to realize the negative health impact that a collapse in social structures can have. A world-renowned cardiologist, Dean Ornish, had this to say when speaking about the underlying causes of heart disease:

"The real epidemic in our culture is not only physical heart disease, but … *spiritual heart disease* — that is, the profound feelings of loneliness, isolation, alienation, and depression that are so prevalent in our culture with the breakdown of the social structures that used to provide us with a sense of connection and community" (emphasis added).

The social structures that historically connect us with God and community are the church and the family, both introduced in Genesis! Here are some well-known benefits for those who trust in God and fellowship with others through regular church attendance:

- Lower death rates than non-churchgoers — regardless of risk factors
- Fewer symptoms and better health outcomes in 7 of 8 cancer studies, 4 of 5 blood pressure studies, 4 of 6 heart disease studies, and 4 of 5 general health studies
- Less prone to depression, suicide, alcoholism, and other addictions
- A 53 percent quicker recovery from depression
- Three times more likely to survive open-heart surgery
- Hospital stays more than two times shorter than older patients without a religious affiliation
- Stronger immune system function.

The answer is a resounding yes! Studies indicate that churches that have a high regard for Bible health principles found in the Old and New Testaments do the best in these areas.

No wonder the Bible says, "My son, forget not my law; but let thine heart keep my commandments: For length of days, and long life, and peace, shall they add to thee" (Proverbs. 3:1, 2).

Faith Plus Community

Think these benefits can be explained by social support alone? According to the researchers, social support could account for only 15 percent of the effect. In another study involving two groups living in kibbutzim (Jewish commune) in Israel, one secular, one religious, persons living in religious kibbutzim had less illness and a 50 percent lower mortality rate than those living in even tightly knit secular kibbutzim!

So trusting in God does make a big difference!

Conversely, living without faith in God can also cause a negative impact on health. For two years, 444 older patients were followed after their discharge from the hospital. When surveyed, those who wondered "whether or not God had abandoned them" or "if He loved them" had a 20 to 30 percent increase in early mortality as compared to those who had a strong trust in God's love.

So compelling is the evidence for the "faith factor" that even prestigious medical journals like the *Archives of Internal Medicine* have developed spiritual questionnaires to assess a patient's level of trust in God. Science indeed has recognized what every person of faith has known intuitively for centuries — trusting God can be very beneficial to your health!

Finding Health in Faith

You might be thinking, "I'm open to being involved in spiritual things and in church, but amid the vast kaleidoscope of religions and denominations to choose from, do some have teachings that are more helpful to health and longevity than others?"

Amazing Health Fact

Nearly 80 percent of Americans believe spiritual faith and prayer can help people recover from illness or injury. In a survey of 269 doctors in the American Academy of Family Physicians, 99 percent said religious beliefs can contribute to healing. When asked about personal experiences, 63 percent said God had intervened to improve their own medical conditions.

And, "The fear of the LORD is the beginning of wisdom: and the knowledge of the holy is understanding. For by me thy days shall be multiplied, and the years of thy life shall be increased" (Proverbs. 9:10, 11).

Amazing Health Fact

In November 2005, *National Geographic* reported that Seventh-day Adventists in Loma Linda, California, have been scientifically documented as the longest living group in the United States. Their unique longevity has been attributed to two principle causes: First, most Adventists eat a plant-based (vegetarian) diet as outlined in Genesis 1:29. Surprisingly, the second main cause given for their longevity and health was their regular practice of rest, worship, and fellowship every seventh day, which is also found in Genesis 2:2, 3.

Never-ending Health

The most wonderful news of all is that the biblical benefits of a longer, stronger life need not end with a funeral. While the Scriptures declare that "the wages of sin is death," God earnestly desires to offer you forgiveness and a gift of "eternal life" (Romans 6:23).

That life without end can begin for you right now — and will continue forever in a world where there is no more sickness, pain, or death (Revelation 21:4).

Two thousand years ago, God's Son came to earth as a man. He spent His life healing, feeding, and teaching others how they could have eternal life. He perfectly demonstrated the love of God in His life and taught people how to love each other.

His name was Jesus.

Because He was a threat to the religious and political establishment, He was arrested. After a hasty, irregular trial, He was beaten and crucified. Though innocent, Jesus willingly suffered and died to take the punishment for the sins of all mankind. Whoever believes in the life and sacrifice of God's Son can have all their sins forgiven and receive the gift of everlasting life.

Do you want this gift of eternal life and health? You can receive it right now. Wherever you are reading these words, eternal life can begin for

you this moment — all you have to do is start by accepting God's amazing gift and believing in the mission of His Son.

If so, say a simple prayer like the following:

> Dear Lord, I thank you for your wonderful offer of forgiveness and eternal salvation. I freely admit that I've sinned, that I've done things that have hurt You, others, and my own body and mind. I ask that you would forgive me of these sins and that You would cleanse me and give me a new heart and the gift of eternal life. I want to live my life according to Your words and will. I am now putting my faith in You. Thank you for offering your Son, Jesus, to take the penalty for all my sins and hearing and answering this prayer. In His name, I pray. Amen.

Now that you have accepted Christ, you are like a newborn beginning a new spiritual life with Him. Here is the advice that Scripture gives to those who have just accepted Jesus: "As newborn babes, desire the pure milk of the word, that you may grow thereby" (1 Peter 2:2).

Would you like to continue learning how to improve your physical and spiritual health — and live a longer, stronger life? Then take the next step and sign up now for absolutely FREE Bible lessons that will take you even deeper into the incredible life-giving wonders of God's Word.

Just turn to page 29 to get the details on how to take advantage of this FREE offer today! ■

BIBLES | THE BEST GIFT FOR EVERYONE IN THE FAMILY!

Perfect as a gift or for your own personal or group studies. Wide selection to fit any budget!

Personalize your Bibles for just $15 ea. (non-refundable).

A Giant Print Premium Leather: **BK-PSBGPL ... $99.98**

B Genuine Leather: **BK-PSBPL ... $89.98**

C Teal Leathersoft: **BK-PSBTL ... $76.98**

D Brown Leathersoft: **BK-PSBSD ... $76.98**

E Navy Leathersoft: **BK-PSBNL ... $76.98**

F Black Leathersoft: **BK-PSBDB ... $76.98**

G Hardcover: **BK-PSBHR ... $29.95 | 12+ 24.98 ea**

NKJV Prophecy Study Bibles

Amazing Facts. Packed with powerful, inspiring study aids to deepen your understanding of God's Word, our beautiful Prophecy Study Bibles include the following features:

- All 27 Amazing Facts Study Guides
- Explanations of Bible numbers and symbols
- 64-page concordance
- Eight pages of maps
- The Biblical Cyclopedic Index
- Words of Christ in Red
- End-of-text references
- Chronology of the Old Testament
- Harmony of the Gospels
- The Parables and Miracles of Jesus
- Doug Batchelor's "How to Study the Bible"
- And much more!

COOKBOOKS & HEALTH

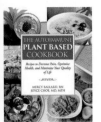

The Autoimmune Plant Based Cookbook: Recipes to Decrease Pain, Optimize Health, and Maximize Your Quality of Life
Wholeness for Life. Expert advice, meal planning, and recipes for implementing an anti-inflammatory lifestyle and taking back your life!
BK-AICB … $24.98

Simply Fresh
Kylee Melo. Plant-based cookbook with lifestyle information and over 75 recipes to improve your health!
BK-SFCB … $24.98

From Plant to Plate: Diabetes Edition
Tami Bivens. Contains over 92 plant-based recipes with corresponding online videos.
BK-PTPD … $19.98

From Plant to Plate
Tami Bivens. Everything a busy person needs to prepare healthy, plant-based meals. Includes QR codes to short, helpful cooking videos.
BK-FPTP … $19.98

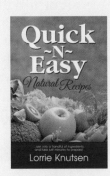

Quick-N-Easy Natural Recipes
Lorrie Knutsen. Simple, healthy, plant-based recipes with five or fewer ingredients—and most take only minutes to prepare!
BK-QENR … $3.98

'Til We Eat Again
Kristina Trajkov. Proceeds from this international vegetarian cookbook help provide quality medical treatment in one of the world's poorest regions.
BK-TWEA … $15.95 Sale $7.75

The Kick Diabetes Cookbook
Brenda Davis. Provides a blueprint for what to eat to defeat diabetes and offers 100 quick-and-easy recipes that are delicious and satisfying!
BK-KDC … $19.98

The Revive Cafe Cookbook 6
Jeremy Dixon. Healthy, whole food, plant-based, gluten-free cooking made easy! This volume features 80 incredible recipes—with a focus on dessert and baking.
BK-RC6 … $19.98

The Revive Cafe Cookbook 7
Jeremy Dixon. From New Zealand's renowned Revive Cafes, this new volume features 81 vegan, gluten-free, whole-food, plant-based recipes that your family will love, including 13 vegan cheese recipes!
BK-RC7 … $19.98

The Brain Health Revolution: Optimal Mental Performance for Life DVD
David DeRose. Enhance your brain performance without relying on drugs or expensive therapies!
DV-BHR … $19.98

The Natural Remedies Encyclopedia
Harvestime Books. One of the most comprehensive, trustworthy books you'll find on natural, drug-free remedies. 1,224 pages!
BK-NRE … $59.98

Visit **AFBOOKSTORE**.COM or call **800-538-7275** to order or learn more.

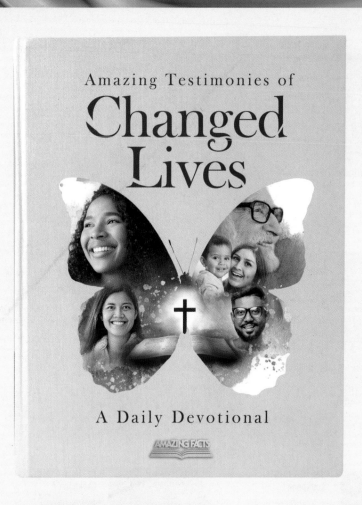

Amazing Testimonies of Changed Lives: A Daily Devotional

Amazing Facts. Be inspired by stories of lives transformed by the love and power of Jesus! Each day of the year, you'll read an uplifting Bible verse and story from a real-life Amazing Facts testimony, Bible character, or historical figure to deepen your walk with God.

Leathersoft | BK-CLDD ... $19.95
Hardcover | BK-CLDH ... $19.95

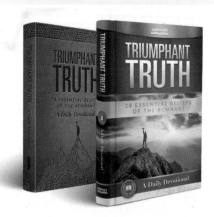

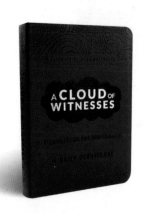

AMAZING FACTS' BESTSELLING DEVOTIONAL!

Triumphant Truth: A Daily Devotional
Amazing Facts. Reflect deeply on the 28 fundamental beliefs of God's remnant church and be prepared to share these vital truths for our times.
Leathersoft | BK-TTDDL ... $19.95
Hardcover | BK-TTDD ... $24.95
NEW LOWER PRICE ... $17.95

A Cloud of Witnesses: A Daily Devotional
Amazing Facts. Discover vast treasures from God's Word revealed through the lives of 258 fascinating Bible characters—and learn priceless life lessons from their spiritual victories and failures.
BK-ACOW ... $14.95

Moving Mountains: A Daily Devotional
Amazing Facts. Get back to the Bible and discover God's creative, powerful voice through compelling, fun, and imaginative daily readings.
BK-MMDD ... $14.95